THE WAY OF KINDNESS
READINGS FOR A GRACEFUL LIFE

THE WAY OF KINDNESS

READINGS FOR
A GRACEFUL LIFE

Michael Leach, James T. Keane,
Doris Goodnough, editors

ORBIS BOOKS
Maryknoll, New York 10545

ORBIS BOOKS
Maryknoll, New York 10545

Fathers and Brothers
MARYKNOLL™

Second Printing, November 2018

Founded in 1970, Orbis Books endeavors to publish works that enlighten the mind, nourish the spirit, and challenge the conscience. The publishing arm of the Maryknoll Fathers and Brothers, Orbis seeks to explore the global dimensions of the Christian faith and mission, to invite dialogue with diverse cultures and religious traditions, and to serve the cause of reconciliation and peace. The books published reflect the views of their authors and do not represent the official position of the Maryknoll Society. To learn more about Maryknoll and Orbis Books, please visit our website at www.maryknollsociety.org.

Copyright © 2018 by Orbis Books.

Published by Orbis Books, Maryknoll, New York 10545–0302.

All rights reserved.

Sources and acknowledgments on pages 248–252 represent an extension of this copyright page.

No part of this publication may be reproduced or transmitted in any form or by any means, electronic or mechanical, including photocopying, recording or any information storage or retrieval system, without prior permission in writing from the publisher.

Queries regarding rights and permissions should be addressed to:
Orbis Books, P.O. Box 302, Maryknoll, New York 10545–0302.

Manufactured in the United States of America.
Design: Roberta Savage

Library of Congress Cataloging-in-Publication Data

Names: Leach, Michael, 1940- editor.
Title: The way of kindness : readings for a graceful life / Michael Leach,
 James T. Keane, Doris Goodnough, editors.
Description: Maryknoll : Orbis Books, 2018. | Includes bibliographical
 references and index. |
Identifiers: LCCN 2017054907 (print) | LCCN 2017059636 (ebook) | ISBN
 9781608337415 (e-book) | ISBN 9781626982758 (pbk.)
Subjects: LCSH: Kindness--Religious aspects--Christianity.
Classification: LCC BV4647.K5 (ebook) | LCC BV4647.K5 W39 2018 (print) |
DDC
 241/.4--dc23
LC record available at https://lccn.loc.gov/2017054907

Three things in human life are important.
The first is to be kind. The second is to be kind.
And the third is to be kind.

—Henry James

CONTENTS

Contents

The Way of Kindness

Contents

The Way of Kindness

Contents

The Way of Kindness

Contents

The Way of Kindness

Kindly Light

Kurt Vonnegut

INTRODUCTION

Imagine a world without kindness. Sometimes you think it's getting that way, don't you? But you know better.

This book is all about kindness, about a world of goodness and love that glows from within no matter the shadows that exist right now. It is filled with true stories and reflections by writers you know and others you will be happy to meet. The purpose is to reassure you that you are on the right track by having made kindness a priority in your life, to recognize that you are in wonderful company, and to be grateful and glad that life is good.

The way of kindness is a mode of being in world that is tender yet fearless—one that brings peace and joy to the giver as well as to the receiver. It is a habit that increases and multiplies. Often at once. Smile at someone and you know. Kindness always reproduces itself. It is a spiritual alchemy that turns shadow to light.

We hope *The Way of Kindness* encourages you to

be aware of moments when kindness calls your name, and inspires you to be grateful for the kindnesses that have graced and continue to grace your own life.

The poet Rumi reminded us that "We are all just walking each other home."

Michael Leach, James T. Keane, Doris Goodnough

Be Kind

Michael Blumenthal

Not merely because Henry James said
there were but four rules of life—
be kind be kind be kind be kind—but
because it's good for the soul, and,
what's more, for others, it may be
that kindness is our best audition
for a worthier world, and, despite
the vagueness and uncertainty of
its recompense, a bird may yet wander
into a bush before our very houses,
gratitude may not manifest itself in deeds
entirely equal to our own, still there's
weather arriving from every direction,
the feasts of famine and feasts of plenty
may yet prove to be one, so why not
allow the little sacrificial squinches and

squigulas to prevail? Why not inundate
the particular world with minute particulars?
Dust's certainly all our fate, so why not
make it the happiest possible dust,
a detritus of blessedness? Surely
the hedgehog, furling and unfurling
into its spiked little ball, knows something
that, with gentle touch and unthreatening
tone, can inure to our benefit, surely the wicked
witches of our childhood have died and,
from where they are buried, a great kindness
has eclipsed their misdeeds. Yes, of course,
in the end so much comes down to privilege
and its various penumbras, but too much
of our unruly animus has already been
wasted on reprisals, too much of the
unblessed air is filled with smoke from
undignified fires. Oh friends, take
whatever kindness you can find
and be profligate in its expenditure:
It will not drain your limited resources,
I assure you, it will not leave you vulnerable
and unfurled, with only your sweet little claws
to defend yourselves, and your wet little noses,
and your eyes to the ground, and your little feet.

Destination Kindness

Anne Lamott

Maps can change a life, a person, returning us to dreams, to our childhood, to the poetic, to what is real. They can move us forward to what we didn't even know we were looking for. A map can change a god-awful day or month, ruin a rut, give us directions home and to everywhere else, near and far, to the golden past and today, to the center and then back to the periphery, to our true selves, our lost selves, the traveler, the mystic, the child, the artist. The point of life, a friend said, is not staying alive, but staying in love, and maps give us a shot at this, taking us to the wild brand-new, the old favorite, and back home. Love, maps, nature, and books are all we have to take us out of time—along with, of course, drugs and shopping, which do the job way more quickly.

Too often we choose the latter, or at least I do, in the dark isolated night of the soul or a bright mess with someone dear. If we stayed in the pain, there would be insight, maybe spiritual progress, but who has the time? Google search Cost Plus, MapQuest, IKEA. Go buy a lamp, some candles. Let there be light.

A few years ago, within the same week I landed in two of the strangest, most incongruous places on earth—the local Zoologie franchise, for your upscale bohemian professional woman, and Hiroshima.

I won't say Zoologie was harder, but it made me feel more acutely that the world is going to hell, so let me begin there.

It is a destination store selling boho-chic clothes and housewares that describes itself as a lifestyle brand that imparts a sense of beauty, optimism, and discovery to the customer. This was two days after I had exchanged horrible words with my son, after a month of mutually held breath, when we both had seen the worst of the other and ourselves. My every attempt at white-flag waving was shot down, so I went to Zoologie to escape, to wallow, to move from agitation to animated trance.

Also, I needed a cute sweater for Japan, where my

Jesuit friend Tom and I were headed in a few days. We had many reasons for going, mostly that we like to travel together, and two main destinations: the church where my grandfather was a minister in the 1920s and 1930s in Tokyo, where my father was born and raised; and Hiroshima. Nights would be cool, and I might need a light wrap.

Thus my field trip to Zoologie. I felt lost in the commercial, the anonymous, the corporate, the lovely scent. Luckily there was a map on the wall. It was a beautiful golden antique map, the kind your grandparents might have used, and it put me in a spending frame of mind: it would look great in my study. I dragged myself away to the blouse racks. There was an incredibly pretty T-shirt that I desperately needed, for only eighty-nine dollars. Sigh: who was it who said that to get into heaven, you needed a letter of recommendation from the poor? What a buzzkill. The clothes really were beautiful. They would definitely help you feel better about yourself, and would almost certainly help you get laid this week. I shook my head to clear it.

Things are not the problem. Things are sometimes the only solution to existential dread, and the five Buddhist remembrances: I am sure to become old; I cannot avoid aging. I am sure to become ill; I cannot avoid illness. I am sure to die; I cannot avoid death. I must be separated and parted from all that is dear and beloved to me. I am the owner of my actions; I cannot escape the consequences of my actions. Except, I might add as a nice Christian girl, through mercy—and things.

There are the things we need to stay alive, and the more numerous things we acquire to feel better about ourselves, more festive things. People have always made things as craft, as creative expression, and bartered for them with one another. Consumerism is not a bad thing, it's very human. But in these high-end retail stores, we are prisoners, which is not so great; these kinds of stores give slavering a good name. Consumerism feels great while we're still in the store—the enchantment, the potential for change, the promise of vast improvement. The store is a temple festooned with our most treasured symbols, those that make us ache for an easier time, the world of childhood, when we were seeing things for the first time, and the magic of that hadn't worn off. What's wrong with this, aside from its being expensive, squandering our time and money, distracting us from life, and wearing off?

I'm easily seduced, a drowsy sitting duck. Zoologie

pimps off the ineffable poetic impulses that the artist Joseph Cornell evoked in his dream boxes, shadow boxes with antique silverware, maps, feathers, and shards of pottery. Zoologie's ambience creates this with similar images of old brooches, children playing, stars, doorknobs, and the ephemeral. It's like an ATM version of Yeats's golden apples of the sun, silver apples of the moon.

And wandering the racks, wishing my son would call, I felt even more vulnerable to the promise of the ephemeral. I so wanted to change reality. One of our aged saints at St. Andrew, my church, who had the hardest life, also had the deepest faith, and no matter what happened in her life she would say, "I know my change is gonna come." I wanted to believe that now. My son had texted earlier to say I didn't trust or support him. I texted that this was completely untrue; it was just that perhaps I was a bit worried about his future. I was charged with being controlling. Moi?

He said, "You're too anxious for me to deal with." He knows where the cracks in my turtle shell are.

To have texted, "You might be right," would have been wonderful aikido. Sadly, this did not cross my mind. I had pled for mercy and forgiveness. Silence. I didn't want to sit at home with my depressing used furniture, used drawer pulls, and used dogs.

I tried to will myself into feeling more merciful toward him: Many times when he was an older teenager, I marveled that I hadn't killed him in his sleep, not because he hadn't deserved it—trust me on this— but because I didn't deserve it, either. God wouldn't have a hard time finding plenty of examples from my own life when I was just as awful, if perhaps a bit less mouthy. Pride prevents us from admitting this, which also prevents its healing. As well as we know our grown children and relatives, we don't know how much energy they have to put into simply keeping their lives together at all. We try to come from a place of mercy because it is good practice; no one is very good at it, especially when someone doesn't deserve it and knows exactly which of our buttons to push.

People try to goad you into seeing that hostile actions are far more a reflection of the hurt the antagonist is feeling than pettiness or meanness of spirit. This is not always helpful, as now you have two resentments. What does help is to pretend to have gotten over the injury—acting as if—and then radical self-care: M&M's, for instance, or shopping.

The right cardigan would lift my spirits, if not heal me of a lifelong isolation, an existential homesickness. Carl Jung said that most painful issues can't be solved—they can only be outgrown, but that takes time and deep work. Nothing in our culture allows us to do that anymore: Don't sit with pain! Go to eBay, the gym, Facebook, Zoologie. Outside, the world is in such a frenzy, megabyte-driven, alien, dehumanizing.

Zoologie smells like childhood would have smelled if you'd had a better family. It is transfixing, like the Sirens. I love their silky voices. They sing to me, whereas almost everything poetic has been squeezed out of the world. But it appears to be alive in here, in the blink of an eye, while with poetry, you have to take your time and meander. Jeez, what a waste of time.

At the makeup display, apparently all I had to do was apply a light new foundation, from a beautiful bottle, to become dewy again in just minutes. How great. But two small problems existed: For one, I was last dewy at ten years old. And two, even I know that real things take real time. Still, I used the tester. The makeup highlighted my wrinkles, settled into the lines beside my mouth, like ink. I looked like I'd been hennaed at a street fair.

I found a cotton cardigan, perfect for Japan, lilac with light green buttons. Even the coat hanger from which it hung created feelings of longing in me. Maybe it was the equivalent of the drug soma in *Brave New World*, but I always thought that sounded good. Every inch of space in the store that was authentic and dreamlike was being used against me, for consumer manipulation. So what—you spend an hour with a sense of gentle touch, meaning, authenticity, connection, an earlier time, a slower, gentler time. How can that be wrong?

But it wasn't working: despite my best efforts to be merciful and unruffled, I was too unsettled. It's rock bottom for me when my son and I are at odds, in self-esteem and confidence. And God loves rock bottom. God was trumping Zoologie. I felt a hollowness, a racing heart, a jaw-sagging disbelief, because I had no answer, whereas I almost always have an answer for everything.

This was the rosary of loss. My son, my youth, my parents, a best friend, the last boyfriend, all gone.

Is there anything that can help at rock bottom? No. Only a friend.

I dialed, and she was there, my old friend who has even more problems than I, and she listened; she got it. That was all. I sighed. This is the greatest mercy I know, a loved one hearing and nodding, even if over the phone. Thomas Merton said, "No matter how low you may have fallen in your own esteem, bear in mind that if you delve deeply into yourself you will discover holiness there." But this is not my experience. I find silt and mental problems. My only hope is to delve deeply into a friend.

She said, "Put the sweater down." I did. "Now back away slowly." I walked across the store to the world's cutest rattan chair, that would look so fabulous in my bedroom. I plopped down and listened to my friend's voice. It was clear, cool water on a sunburn. After a while, one of the thin salesgirls came by. I thought for a moment it was to get me back on my feet to shop, like in *They Shoot Horses, Don't They?*, the movie about a Depression-era dance marathon. When I told my friend this, she said, "You may be too far gone this time." I had to laugh. I looked at the woman. Up close she looked about twenty, innocent beneath a thick layer of makeup, while I felt so old and crazy. Did she have the map back home?

No, but she had brought me the tiniest paper cup of water, like one you might serve to a cat. I received it. That's the hard part, not taking but receiving. She turned away, so friendly and content, while I was so off. What did she have that I didn't, beside beauty and youth? I thought, and thought, and then I almost smote my own forehead: She had kindness. She was doing kind things, helping people. The map is kind action. If people are patient and kind, that's a lot— something of the spirit is at work. The result of grace. It doesn't come naturally. What comes naturally is, Shoot the mother. So I decided to be like the salesgirl when I grew up, patient, friendly, kind. I got off the phone. In two minutes, I was happy.

And I suddenly understood that Jung would have loved this ridiculous place with all its symbols. Oh, honey, he'd have said, we're just silly fools. We can laugh at ourselves. We have to. We have to harvest humility. Who do we think we are? Rats who are into cosmetics. He'd say, You don't need this. We'll pull through. You're going to be okay. Let's sit down right here on this Flutter Pattern Dream Menagerie Rug, and write a poem together.

I still didn't know how things with my son would bounce. I have a quote taped to my office wall from an anonymous source that says, "Love is hard. Love is . . . seeing the darkness in another person and defying the impulse to jump ship." I prayed for both of us. And now there was some visible mercy, in the teeny cup of water and in my friend's helping me off the hook of trying to fix the unfixable. I was free again, ish; back on the ground with tired feet instead of with one on a sailboat pulling away, where I might fall into the drink. I was dry and loved. It was a glut of mercy, actually. There are so many ways for a life to go bad, for a person to end up permanently isolated, thwarted, blaming. I had genetic and cultural preconditions for just such a life. But instead, I had a great friend and a sip of water. Also, in a way I can't account for, which had nothing to do with what I knew or thought I could manage, I had found an off-the-beaten-track means to a redeemed life, with friends whose love saves me. The odds were so against it that I can only call it mercy.

It brought me home. I accidentally bought the sweater on my way out.

❖ ❖ ❖

A week or so later, wearing my light lilac sweater, I went with Tom to see the neighborhood in Tokyo where my father lived from 1923 until 1938, the son of Presbyterian missionaries, God's frozen chosen, and the reason my father so loathed Christianity. I wanted to see my grandparents' church, where my grandfather taught, where they worshipped, where my father and aunt were children. Tom, who can read foreign subway maps, had gotten us to the hilariously nondescript church in my dad's formerly crummy neighborhood, which was basically now Rodeo Drive, except for the church.

People say that expectations are resentments under construction, and even though I have found that to be true, I had high expectations of my welcome at my grandfather's church. I thought the ministers would be amazed at my intergenerational story. But the Japanese ministers I explained myself to were friendly, important, and busy.

They kind of blew me off. What had I expected? "Oh my God, we named our kids after your grandfather!" Or, "Thank God for white people."

I laughed and said to God, "Thank you for getting me here, with my dear and cranky friend." Talk about anticlimactic. But because of God, Tom, grace, and a map from our hotel, I got there, to my grandfather's church.

❖❖❖

Two days later, we were at a small lecture hall in Hiroshima, and I was reading a poem that a Japanese girl had written two weeks after the bomb blast in 1945.

Her teenage sister was dying; she and her mom went to the market to buy the sister tomatoes, but while they were gone, the sister died. An ancient, very sweet survivor in a kimono had read the poem to a dozen of us guests at the end of her presentation, movie footage of the bombing and its aftermath. Then she bowed to us and flutteringly asked if one of us would read it to her and our group. I had no idea why, but because it was absurd and charming, when no one else volunteered, I did. She nodded encouragingly as I read, as if we were at a piano recital. It made as much sense as anything does here, her polite inclusion. Polite inclusion is the gateway drug to mercy.

We had taken the bullet train from Kyoto. Tom was even more cranky than usual, because his feet and hands hurt, and he would not admit he was hungry; also, it was a bit cold for people who had forgotten sweaters. I had a broken toe and a healthful snack of toasted soybeans, and was wearing a walking boot but trying not to mind my toe or Tom, although I felt put upon by his mood. I was pretty sure, as usual, that if he had done what I had had the sense to do— snack, sweater—he could just snap out of it. Then we would have a rich and touching day at this most astonishing war memorial. Life would be better for almost everyone. What is so scary is that I live by this belief. Tom, who doesn't, was distant, quiet, and watchful.

Peace Memorial Park can do that to you. It was built in a field created by the explosion, where once had been the center of a bustling city. Little Boy, the bomb dropped on Hiroshima, had been our best thinking at the time. Now drones are our best thinking, and Botox.

You can't help thinking of drones when you see the Children's Peace Monument, a statue of a girl holding a paper crane, which is surrounded by willows and ginkgo trees, the latter called "bearers of hope" because six survived the blast and later bloomed. Hiroshima was a logical outcome of racism, oppression, organized violence, camps. When it starts, there's no containing it. Just over a decade ago we thought, Oh, we'll have a nice war, and all be home for Christmas. We won't have a single bad day, and it will pay for itself. Then we couldn't stop it.

I waited for Tom to catch up, and we headed down to the river. And there we saw something that shocked us into joy, full presence, into blown-away: a dock full of Hawaiian folksingers, in aloha regalia and leis, slack-key guitarists and small children, all singing to the people of Japan.

These first Americans attacked by the Japanese had been welcomed by and were singing to the first people in the world whom Americans had bombed with a nuclear weapon. It stopped me. It gentled me. This is one meaning of meek, as in Blessed are—gentled like wild horses in benevolent experienced hands.

Thirty or so people, Western tourists and Japanese women and girls in kimonos, men in business suits and sweats, Asian youth in hip-hop gear, all stood gaping, immobilized. No pieces to move around our board games, no random bluster or grievance, just notes of a song, and harmonies.

My grandfather's church got me to the Hawaiian folksingers at the dock in Hiroshima. And the atomic bomb that we dropped there is probably the reason my father, who fought on Okinawa, lived. But there was not much life in Hiroshima when America was done. Afterward, we thoughtfully rebuilt Japan, and fed her people, because there was nothing left. There was virtually no rice harvest. We built shelter, infrastructure. Of course we also held some trials and hung some people, so there was that. But for now, today, the folksingers sang. All is change. I don't love this: it is very hard to bear most of the time, but wasn't that day. After a long while, the singers took a final bow, and turned to give hugs to the Japanese helpers on the dock, and then those of us onshore. Thank God I am in charge of so little, or this could never have happened; life is much wilder, richer, and more profound than I am comfortable with. Tom looked at his watch. It was time to go to the lecture hall, where we would find the ancient Japanese woman to whom I would read a child's poem about tomatoes. We located the nearby hall on our Peace Park map and headed off. We got lost, and young people who did not speak English pointed the way. We discover mercy in the smallest moments of kindness and attention and amazement, at our own crabby stamina, at grandmas in kimonos and babies in leis, at willow trees in a park turning from green to gold to red.

Kindly Lights

A good heart . . . a heart like a house.
—Irwin Shaw

Constant kindness can accomplish much.
As the sun makes ice melt,
kindness causes misunderstanding,
mistrust, and hostility to evaporate.
— Albert Schweitzer

Kindness and compassion toward all living things
is a mark of a civilized society. Conversely, cruelty,
whether it is directed against human beings or
against animals, is not the exclusive province of
any one culture or community of people. Racism,
economic deprival, dog fighting and cock fighting,
bull fighting and rodeos are cut from the same

fabric: violence. Only when we have become non-violent toward all life will we have learned to live well ourselves.

—CESAR CHAVEZ

Imagine what our real neighborhoods would be like if each of us offered as a matter of course, just one kind word to another person. . . . One kind word has a wonderful way of turning into many.

—FRED ROGERS

3

Memories of Unkindness

Joan Chittister

*Once a brother committed a sin in Scetis, and the elders
assembled and sent for Abba Moses. He, however, did not
want to go. Then the priest sent a message to him, saying:
"Come, everybody is waiting for you." So he finally got
up to go. And he took a worn-out basket with holes, filled
it with sand, and carried it along. The people who came
to meet him said: "What is this?" Then the old man said:
"My sins are running out behind me, yet I do not see them.
And today I have come to judge the sins of someone else."
When they heard this, they said nothing to the brother and
pardoned him.*

The desert monastics are clear: Self-righteousness
is cruelty done in the name of justice. It is conceiv-
able, of course, that we might find a self-righteous religious. It is feasible that we, like Abba Moses, could

certainly find a self-righteous cleric. It is probable that I might very well find myself dealing with a self-righteous friend or neighbor or even family member. But it is not possible to find a self-righteous contemplative. Not a real contemplative.

Contemplation breaks us open to ourselves. The fruit of contemplation is self-knowledge, not self-justification. "The nearer we draw to God," Abba Mateos said, "the more we see ourselves as sinners." We see ourselves as we really are, and knowing ourselves we cannot condemn the other. We remember with a blush the public sin that made us mortal. We recognize with dismay the private sin that curls within us in fear of exposure. Then the whole world changes when we know ourselves. We gentle it. The fruit of self-knowledge is kindness. Broken ourselves, we bind tenderly the wounds of the other.

The most telling measure of the meaning of kindness in life is memories of unkindness in our own: scenes from a childhood marked by the cruelty of other children, recollections of disdain that scarred the heart, moments of scorn or rejection that leave a person feeling marginalized in the human community. In those moments of isolation we remember the impact of the fracturing of hope. We feel again the pain that comes with the assault on the sliver of dignity that refuses to die in us, however much the degradation of the moment. It is then that we come to understand that kindness, compassion, understanding, acceptance is the irrefutable mark of holiness because we ourselves have known—or perhaps have never known—the balm of kindness for which we so desperately thirsted in those situations. Kindness is an act of God that makes the dry dust of rejection digestible to the human psyche.

Cruelty is not the fruit of contemplation. Those who have touched the God who lives within themselves, with all their struggles, all their lack, see God everywhere and, most of all, in the helpless, fragile, pleading, frightened other. Contemplatives do not judge the heart of another by a scale on which they themselves could not be vindicated.

The pitfall of the religion of perfection is self-righteousness, that cancer of the soul that requires more of others than it demands of itself and so erodes its own fiber even more. It is an inner blindness that counts the sins of others but has no eye for itself. The self-righteous soul, the soul that preens on its own virtue, denies itself the self-knowledge that enables God to ignore what is lacking in us because our hearts are on the right way. It blocks the spirit of life from filling up the gaps within us that we ourselves are helpless to repair because the soul is not ready to receive.

Real contemplatives receive the other with the open arms of God because they have come to know that for all their emptiness God has received them.

To be a contemplative it is necessary to take in without reservation those whom the world casts out because it is they who show us most clearly the face of the waiting God.

4

My Acts of Kindness Always Yield Craziness

Amy Morris-Young

When my husband Dan and I started dating, and we were getting to know each other, one of the first memorable things he said to me was: "You are generous to a fault."

I remember focusing my etch-glass laser Catholic lady stare on him. I had a bunch of retorts swimming in my head, such as: All my bills get paid first. My kids get fed and clothed first. I never give more than what is left over.

But what I said was: "I know. I can't help it."

Because he was right, in a way. I sensed that trying to explain my compulsion to give stuff or money away would be complicated. It goes so deep in my Irish-Italian Catholic DNA, back through 16 years of Catholic school, it is as much a part of me as my eye color or loud laugh or need to drop off a lasagna dinner when someone is sick or hurt.

It is hard to talk about this, as it sounds like I am tooting my own horn, which is the opposite of what giving should be. But never fear: each and every kind act of my life seems to have been written by Woody Allen.

Something inevitably goes wrong. I am pretty sure God does this so we never get to feel too good about ourselves. I am always humbler and stupider after doing something nice. That's the deal, how I know all is right with the world.

In the 1969 movie *Take the Money and Run*, Allen plays Virgil the bank robber who hands a hastily-written hold-up note to the teller. They quibble over whether the word is "Gun" or "Gub" . . . and the next scene finds Virgil in jail.

This is how all my acts of kindness invariably go.

But even knowing that I am bound at the very least to make a total fool of myself and at most, risk incarceration or some other disaster, I simply can't help myself.

The words from the song "Whatsoever You Do to the Least of my Brothers"—based on the passage from Matthew 25:31–40—start repeating through me like a roll in a player piano, each time I encounter a chance to help.

It is undeniable, and takes me right back to first grade, on my knees, leaning on the altar railing at De La Salle church in Granada Hills, Calif., singing:

When I was hungry you gave me to eat
When I was thirsty you gave me to drink.
Now enter into the home of your Father.
When I was homeless you opened the door
When I was naked you gave me your coat
Now enter into the home of your Father.

That and the song from the Prayer of St. Francis— "Make Me a Channel of your Peace"—do me in, every time.

For example, once I was walking from the parking lot to my office on a snowy day. I was wearing a warm knitted cap, scarf and mittens. I had a couple of extra pairs of those cheap $2 mittens from the drug store in my backpack. I kept a whole drawer of them at home, as my three kids were forever losing them.

I saw a woman walking across the street from me, without a coat, wearing a light cotton dress and only a tied bandanna on her head. Her bare hands were bright red.

No-brainer, right? I had three pairs of mittens, she had none. Duh. Roll song.

I crossed the street, digging in my backpack as I went, then stood in front of the lady, holding out a pair of mittens, with a big cheesy smile on my face. Only then did I become aware that she was a recent immigrant from somewhere in Eastern Europe. Her eyes were huge with alarm, and she waved me off, her hands pushing me away.

I insisted, pushing the mittens at her.

She started crying.

Via our horrible mix of English and what I took to be Russian, I somehow figured out that she thought I was accusing her of stealing the mittens.

I pushed them back at her. "No, no, no. These are YOUR mittens! Take them!"

She was nearly hysterical now, looking around for help. Her face clearly telegraphed: "Someone save me from the Insane Mitten Lady!"

Exasperated, I threw the mittens at her. She caught them. I ran as fast as I could across the street, not looking back, ducking into my office building. Welcome to my charitable world.

Or another time, I was walking to the same building and saw a homeless lady sleeping on the lawn, her body partially covered by a blue plastic tarp. The only way I knew she was under there was that one of her hands and some of her gray curly hair stuck out, laying on the damp grass. Again, there goes the music.

I leaned over and tried to slip a $5 bill under the tarp near her limp hand. Suddenly, her dry bony hand grabbed my wrist. She reared out of the tarp like a skinny lion, screaming in my face, accusing me of trying to steal the money from her. I stumbled backwards, untangling our hands, and fell backwards on the wet grass.

Green grass stain down the entire leg of my work pants, check. Angry homeless lady, waving a $5 bill and screaming obscenities at me as I trudge back to my office, check. Another great moment in charity land.

Oscar Wilde famously said: "No good deed goes unpunished."

And while I think he meant to sound worldly and cynical, I have to agree with him—but in a good way.

The point, I hope, is that these moments are not about making me feel better. They are about doing what we can, even when we know it will result in a crazy comedy of errors.

Years ago, I lifted something too heavy on the job

and hurt my neck. It took Labor and Industries a full year to acknowledge that I was not only really hurt—and not faking it—but needed surgery. I was in teeth-chattering pain, my left arm didn't function well, and I could only work about half of the day before I fell asleep on my desk from exhaustion.

Pretty soon, I had used up all my sick leave. I was a single mom with three little kids, and we were limping along on half pay. It was terrifying. And lonely. And desperate.

That Thanksgiving and Christmas, I cried tears of relief when the local Christian church delivered charity boxes to our front porch. Without them, there was no way I could have provided holiday meals for my kids.

My two boys Nick and Duncan were oblivious about from where the sudden gush of groceries came, but my teenaged daughter Chelsea was mortified. She begged me to hide the gift-wrapped boxes of food in our garage, so her friends wouldn't see.

After I recovered from my neck surgery the following spring, I told my kids that from now on, we would always adopt families during the holidays. It was a tangible way to say "thank you" for the generosity that had so helped us, and pay it forward.

But that first Christmas, when my kids and I delivered the wrapped gifts and boxes of groceries to our adopted food bank family, they acted anything but grateful. The mother actually asked us for more money (which I did not have), and better presents.

We piled back into our van, the boys in the back seat, Chelsea in the front with me. As we were driving home, she said: "Well, that is the last time we are doing that!"

I said: "What do you mean?"

She folded her arms. "They were totally ungrateful and mean to us!"

I reached over and touched her leg. "Do you think maybe that Mom was embarrassed?"

Chelsea's eyes narrowed. "Huh?"

I lightly squeezed her leg. "I mean, she never thought she would need to be given charity boxes to give her kids food and gifts? I never did, Chelsea. But it sure happened to us, right?"

She nodded.

"I was embarrassed, too. I thought I would always be the one giving those boxes away, not getting them, you know? But stuff happens. She might feel the same way."

"But," Chelsea's face showed confusion, "You

weren't mean when we got that stuff last year."

I nodded, putting my hand back on the steering wheel. "True. But if there is one thing I have learned about giving, it very rarely is about how good it makes you feel. It is about doing the right thing. Even when it makes you feel mad or bad, yes?"

She sighed. "Well, that's dumb."

"Yes, ma'am," I agreed, "yes, it is."

She smiled then. We both did.

One day, I was out walking with son Nick. As we started across the street at a crosswalk, we almost literally bumped into our neighbor in his van, waiting to turn right. He had his three little kids in the backseat. He rolled down his window to say hello. When I saw his haggard face, I asked what was up.

He explained that he had been hurt on the job, and was awaiting back surgery. He wasn't working much, and was just driving his kids around, trying to give them something to do and cheer them up.

I squeezed his forearm and told him to hang in there.

Nick and I walked back to our car. I drove straight to the market, and no surprise, bought a frozen lasagna, a bag of Caesar salad and a big loaf of garlic bread. I dropped the bag on our friend's front porch on our way home. I sent him a quick text message, alerting him to check on his porch before dinner time.

As we pulled into our driveway, my cellphone lit up with a text message.

It read: "Who is this?"

I texted back: "Amy."

The next text said: "There isn't anything on our front porch."

I wrote back: "What? That's weird. I just left it there."

The answer came: "Oh. We moved."

I looked up at the sky, and smiled.

I texted back, asking for their new address.

I understood fully that I was about to turn around, go back, collect the bag (if it was still there) from a total stranger's front porch, buy a new bag of groceries if it wasn't there, then deliver it to the correct address.

And I knew, without a doubt, that all was right with the world.

5

The Evidence of Kindness

Mother Teresa

The streets of Calcutta were dangerous, dirty, and crowded. People were infected with cholera and leprosy, dysentery and other diseases that were fatal in most cases. Mother Teresa and her group of helpers went among them every day with courage and conviction to do what they could to ease their pain.

One day, Mother Teresa came across a young woman in the gutter of the street, directly in front of one of the Calcutta hospitals. The woman was so ill that she did not notice or care that the rats and cockroaches were eating her feet. Mother picked up the woman and carried her into the hospital. She told the nurse inside:

This woman is dying. She needs help.

But the nurse replied:

Sorry, no room for her here. She is poor and can't pay

and we can't save her anyway, so we can't waste a bed on her. Now please move along.

Mother Teresa's heart broke as she carried the woman back to the street, and there she stayed with the woman for hours until she died. Mother Teresa was angry and she felt like no one should have to die alone, forgotten and in despair in the dirty street.

Mother Teresa found an old abandoned hotel just behind a Hindu temple and started bringing in the people the hospital refused to admit. They were so sick that she knew there was no hope of survival for them, but she felt compelled to make a place they could come to die. It was a horrible undertaking as the people who filled the rooms had open wounds covered with maggots or had parts of their bodies missing due to disease. The Hindus from the Temple did not want these people close to them and threw garbage and rocks at Mother Teresa.

One day, Mother Teresa saw a man lying on the steps of the Hindu temple—very sick. She learned he was one of the Hindu priests and no one at the temple would touch him for fear of getting his disease. So they put him on the steps to die. Mother Teresa picked him up and took him to the old hotel where she cared for him until he died a peaceful death. The

Hindus at the temple saw what she had done and never gave her any trouble again.

Kindly Lights

*Whatever you think people are withholding from
you—praise, appreciation, assistance, loving care,
and so on—give it to them. You don't have it? Just
act as if you had it, and it will come. Then, soon
after you start giving, you will start receiving.
Outflow determines inflow.*

—ECKHART TOLLE

*Just because an animal is large, it doesn't mean
he doesn't want kindness; however big Tigger
seems to be, remember that he wants as much
kindness as Roo.*

—A. A. MILNE (WINNIE-THE-POOH)

*It's a bit embarrassing to have been concerned with
human problems all one's life and find at the end*

*that one has no more to offer by way of advice than
"try to be a little kinder."*

—Aldous Huxley

6

I am sorry. I will never do that again.

Thich Nhat Hanh

In our daily lives, we are often caught by wrong perceptions. We are human, and we make mistakes. When we listen unmindfully, we misunderstand the other person. We have to be aware of that. The Buddha said that we are caught many times a day by our wrong perceptions. We have to be careful not to be too sure of our perceptions. You might like to calligraphy these three words and put them on your wall as a bell of mindfulness:

Are you sure?

When we look deeply, we often discover that it is we who cause ourselves the most suffering. We think our suffering is brought about by others—our parents, our partner, our so-called enemy—but when we look deeply, we see that out of forgetfulness, anger, or jealousy, we have said or done things to create our own suffering and the suffering of those around us. Suppose in the past I said something unkind to someone and made him suffer. Now, touching deeply the present, I can breathe in and out, smile to that person, and say:

I am sorry. I will never do that again.

The importance of saying sorry.

When I practice this, I see the other person smiling to me even if he is not there, even if he has already passed away, and my wound can be healed. Touching the present deeply, we can heal the past. The practice of dwelling in the present moment can help us calm ourselves and transform our pain.

7

Err on the Side of Kindness

George Saunders

So, quick, end-of-speech advice: Since, according to me, your life is going to be a gradual process of becoming kinder and more loving: Hurry up. Speed it along. Start right now. There's a confusion in each of us, a sickness, really: *selfishness*. But there's also a cure. So be a good and proactive and even somewhat desperate patient on your own behalf—seek out the most efficacious anti-selfishness medicines, energetically, for the rest of your life.

Do all the other things, the ambitious things—travel, get rich, get famous, innovate, lead, fall in love, make and lose fortunes, swim naked in wild jungle rivers (after first having it tested for monkey poop)—but as you do, to the extent that you can, *err in the direction of kindness*. Do those things that incline you toward the big questions, and avoid the things that would reduce you and make you trivial. That luminous part of you that exists beyond personality—your soul, if you will—is as bright and shining as any that has ever been. Bright as Shakespeare's, bright as Gandhi's, bright as Mother Teresa's. Clear away everything that keeps you separate from this secret luminous place. Believe it exists, come to know it better, nurture it, share its fruits tirelessly.

And someday, in 80 years, when you're 100, and I'm 134, and we're both so kind and loving we're nearly unbearable, drop me a line, let me know how your life has been. I hope you will say: It has been so wonderful.

Congratulations, Class of 2013.

I wish you great happiness, all the luck in the world, and a beautiful summer.

8

Learning to Love My Neighbor in New York

Kerry Weber

One cold winter night I bought a tuna sandwich for dinner at a pharmacy. I was hungry and late for a meeting and was feeling sorry for myself for having to eat dinner at a place that also sells stockings and cold medicine. I passed a man curled up under some blankets on the street. "Got anything to eat?" he asked, clearly seeing that I did. I took out half of the sandwich and gave it to him. But as I walked away, doubts filled my head: *Should I have given him the whole sandwich? Should I have bought another one just for him? Was he even hungry?*

It's not easy to determine the best ways to act with kindness and mercy. Of course St. Basil the Great, of the fourth century, put it quite simply:

The bread which you do not use is the bread

of the hungry; the garment hanging in your wardrobe is the garment of him who is naked.

... The acts of charity that you do not perform are so many injustices that you commit.

That's a challenging statement. My lack of action can be, in itself, an injustice. But how do we know when and how to act? It seems like too much, sometimes, to feel for every person you see and to give to people in need not knowing what they'll do with the money. It is difficult to see everyone as an individual.

An Expanding Heart

In the summer before that cold winter night, I had been threatened by a man who had locked himself in the wheelchair-accessible bathroom at church. I'd knocked on the door, and the man had emerged, a flurry of baggy, ragged clothes and unkempt hair. Angry, screaming and delusional, he believed his feet had been burned by acid and that I'd been continually bothering him. His arm was raised and his fist clenched tightly as he started at me. All I can remember about that moment is thinking, *I'm about to get punched in the face,* although I made no attempt to move. Sensing this, my then-boyfriend stepped in to mediate, and the man punched him in the face instead. It was a long day.

Since then I'd been a bit more wary of than worried about many of the homeless people I passed on the street, yet I tried to strike a balance between vigilance and mercy. Mercy, as described by Venerable Catherine McAuley, founder of the Sisters of Mercy, is "the principal path pointed out by Jesus Christ to those who are desirous of following Him." It sounds simple enough. And yet I often feel that this path can be a difficult one to travel, and that keeping pace with Jesus, our guide on this path, is a challenge.

The thing is, it's easy to imagine yourself doing great works of mercy. It's easy to have good intentions. What's difficult is the follow-through, because God didn't challenge us to commit to the corporal works of mercy for a few days. God challenges us to commit to a lifestyle—and a lifetime—of mercy. And that's not easy, because maybe in the end, the corporal works of mercy—feeding the hungry, giving drink to the thirsty, sheltering the homeless and others—aren't things that can be completed the way one can finish playing a board game or painting a picture. Each act is not an isolated incident, but a part of a process, akin to sweeping the floor. You have to do it regularly or things begin to get messy. They must become habits without becoming mindless. Ultimately, the works of mercy point us toward ways in which we can build God's reign on earth.

And yet action must be rooted in relationship. In one of the most powerful passages in Dorothy Day's autobiography, *The Long Loneliness,* she speaks of the wonderful evolution of the Catholic Worker movement and writes about how many surprising, God-filled moments came about while "we were just sitting there talking." She writes of people moving in and out of the house and says, "Somehow the walls expanded." I can't help but think that here she writes not only of the willingness of the community to take on and take in guests, but also of the walls of the heart growing in kind. Because that is how our hearts are meant to work: just when you think your heart is full to the point of breaking, it adapts and grows and learns to love more than you ever thought you could.

A Sheltered Life

In an effort to delve more deeply into these works of mercy, I decided to stay as an overnight volunteer at a homeless shelter at a nearby church. I would spend the night in a church basement with more than a dozen men I'd never met, and I had no idea what to expect.

When I arrive, the shelter feels strangely similar, like the kind of place in which I would have attended a Brownie sleepover as a child, but with rough, folded cots instead of thin, Minnie Mouse-themed sleeping bags on the floor. The walls of the shelter are white, and the room is long and sparse. The cots are folded and lined up near the walls; each already has blankets on it. Near each bed are hooks on the walls upon which hang random personal items, presumably owned by the men: a few jackets, a suit coat on one hook; a plastic, gold-colored centurion helmet on another.

When the men arrive, a young man smiles broadly at me and introduces himself as Angelo. He holds out his hand to shake mine. "Don't worry, they're clean," he says. I am not worried about germs, just shocked that he is so young. He couldn't be older than his early twenties. Next, Greg comes over. He is wearing a blue-grey sweatshirt and has several tattoos. We begin chatting, and the subjects range from our favorite kinds of chicken to the fact that he's been to Western Massachusetts, where I grew up.

Greg tells me he has been all over New England and the Midwest. His dad was in the Navy. When he finds out I work for a Jesuit magazine, he says he knew a guy who went to a Jesuit high school. As he talks, he spreads peanut butter on a toasted heel of bread and then rolls it up.

"Are the Jesuits like the brothers up by St. Francis? Is there a rivalry, like gangs?" he asks, laughing.

"Like the Sharks and the Jets," I say. "Lots of finger snapping."

Johnny, who has been sitting nearby, gets up and walks away and then comes back with a card that reads *St. Padre Pío House.* He says it's at 155th Street in the South Bronx. "He was a priest who bled from his hands and feet," he says with a sweet pride at being able to connect my world to his. "Yeah, that's the stigmata," I say. Johnny nods.

A man named Louis asks if I brought earplugs. I tell him no. "I hope you're a good sleeper," he replies. One of the men tells me a joke and I laugh in approval. Greg chimes in, "You have to let her think we're high-quality homeless people," he says and laughs, as well. And in that moment I realized that, deep in conversation, I'd forgotten about that label for a while. I hadn't tried to categorize the men as crazy or Christ-like. I'd just let them be. And I'd allowed myself to be present.

The lights go out at 10:30 p.m., and I have a difficult time falling asleep. Around 11 p.m., a cellphone rings. The snoring is at all volume levels and intervals, so at times it sounds almost like one continuous rumble. I understand now why Louis asked me about the earplugs. A man starts coughing with gusto. Someone brushes off his sheets. And yet somehow, after talking with many of the men that evening, all the noise doesn't really bother me. I'm grateful that they've welcomed me. Throughout the evening, that small space seemed to expand, as the men made sandwiches or watched movies or just sat there talking. I feel surprisingly at home.

Kindly Lights

*No act of kindness, no matter how small, is ever
wasted.*

—Aesop

*The best memory is that which forgets nothing,
but injuries. Write kindness in marble and write
injuries in the dust.*

—Persian Proverb

*Kindness should be the natural way of life, not the
exception.*

—Buddha

*Too often we underestimate the power of a touch, a
smile, a kind word, a listening ear, an honest com-
pliment, or the smallest act of caring, all of which
have the potential to turn a life around.*

—Leo Buscaglia

Masters of Love

Emily Esfahani Smith

Every day in June, the most popular wedding month of the year, about 13,000 American couples will say "I do," committing to a lifelong relationship that will be full of friendship, joy, and love that will carry them forward to their final days on this earth.

Except, of course, it doesn't work out that way for most people. The majority of marriages fail, either ending in divorce and separation or devolving into bitterness and dysfunction. Of all the people who get married, only three in ten remain in healthy, happy marriages, as psychologist Ty Tashiro points out in his book *The Science of Happily Ever After*, which was published earlier this year.

Social scientists first started studying marriages by observing them in action in the 1970s in response to a crisis: Married couples were divorcing at unprece dented rates. Worried about the impact these divorces would have on the children of the broken marriages, psychologists decided to cast their scientific net on couples, bringing them into the lab to observe them and determine what the ingredients of a healthy, lasting relationship were. Was each unhappy family unhappy in its own way, as Tolstoy claimed, or did the miserable marriages all share something toxic in common?

Psychologist John Gottman was one of those researchers. For the past four decades, he has studied thousands of couples in a quest to figure out what makes relationships work. I recently had the chance to interview Gottman and his wife Julie, also a psychologist, in New York City. Together, the renowned experts on marital stability run The Gottman Institute, which is devoted to helping couples build and maintain loving, healthy relationships based on scientific studies.

John Gottman began gathering his most critical findings in 1986, when he set up "The Love Lab" with his colleague Robert Levenson at the University of Washington. Gottman and Levenson brought newlyweds into the lab and watched them interact with each other. With a team of researchers, they hooked the couples up to electrodes and asked the couples to speak about their relationship, like how they met, a major conflict they were facing together, and a positive memory they had. As they spoke, the electrodes measured the subjects' blood flow, heart rates, and how much sweat they produced. Then the researchers sent the couples home and followed up with them six years later to see if they were still together.

From the data they gathered, Gottman separated the couples into two major groups: the *masters* and the *disasters*. The masters were still happily together after six years. The disasters had either broken up or were chronically unhappy in their marriages. When the researchers analyzed the data they gathered on the couples, they saw clear differences between the masters and disasters. The disasters looked calm during the interviews, but their physiology, measured by the electrodes, told a different story. Their heart rates were quick, their sweat glands were active, and their blood flow was fast. Following thousands of couples longitudinally, Gottman found that the more physiologically active the couples were in the lab, the quicker their relationships deteriorated over time.

But what does physiology have to do with anything? The problem was that the disasters showed all the signs of arousal—of being in fight-or-flight mode—in their relationships. Having a conversation sitting next to their spouse was, to their bodies, like facing off with a saber-toothed tiger. Even when they were talking about pleasant or mundane facets of their relationships, they were prepared to attack and be attacked. This sent their heart rates soaring and made them more aggressive toward each other. For example, each member of a couple could be talking about how their days had gone, and a highly aroused husband might say to his wife, "Why don't you start talking about your day. It won't take you very long."

The masters, by contrast, showed low physiological arousal. They felt calm and connected together, which translated into warm and affectionate behavior, even when they fought. It's not that the masters had, by default, a better physiological make-up than the disasters; it's that masters had created a climate of trust and intimacy that made both of them more emotionally and thus physically comfortable.

Gottman wanted to know more about how the masters created that culture of love and intimacy, and how the disasters squashed it. In a follow-up study in 1990, he designed a lab on the University of Washington campus to look like a beautiful bed and breakfast retreat. He invited 130 newlywed couples to spend the day at this retreat and watched them as they did what couples normally do on vacation: cook, clean, listen to music, eat, chat, and hang out. And Gottman made a critical discovery in this study—one that gets at the heart of why some relationships thrive while others languish.

Throughout the day, partners would make requests for connection, what Gottman calls "bids." For example, say that the husband is a bird enthusiast and notices a goldfinch fly across the yard. He might say to his wife, "Look at that beautiful bird outside!" He's not just commenting on the bird here: he's requesting a response from his wife—a sign of interest or support—hoping they'll connect, however momentarily, over the bird.

The wife now has a choice. She can respond by either "turning toward" or "turning away" from her husband, as Gottman puts it. Though the bird-bid might seem minor and silly, it can actually reveal a lot about the health of the relationship. The husband thought the bird was important enough to bring it up in conversation and the question is whether his wife recognizes and respects that.

People who turned toward their partners in the

study responded by engaging the bidder, showing interest and support in the bid. Those who didn't—those who turned away—would not respond or respond minimally and continue doing whatever they were doing, like watching TV or reading the paper. Sometimes they would respond with overt hostility, saying something like, "Stop interrupting me, I'm reading."

These bidding interactions had profound effects on marital well-being. Couples who had divorced after a six-year follow up had "turn-toward bids" 33 percent of the time. Only three in ten of their bids for emotional connection were met with intimacy. The couples who were still together after six years had "turn-toward bids" 87 percent of the time. Nine times out of ten, they were meeting their partner's emotional needs.

❖ ❖ ❖

By observing these types of interactions, Gottman can predict with up to 94 percent certainty whether couples—straight or gay, rich or poor, childless or not—will be broken up, together and unhappy, or together and happy several years later. Much of it comes down to the spirit couples bring to the relationship.

Do they bring kindness and generosity; or contempt, criticism, and hostility?

"There's a habit of mind that the masters have," Gottman explained in an interview, "which is this: they are scanning social environment for things they can appreciate and say thank you for. They are building this culture of respect and appreciation very purposefully. Disasters are scanning the social environment for partners' mistakes."

"It's not just scanning environment," chimed in Julie Gottman. "It's scanning the *partner* for what the *partner* is doing right or scanning him for what he's doing wrong and criticizing versus respecting him and expressing appreciation."

Contempt, they have found, is the number one factor that tears couples apart. People who are focused on criticizing their partners miss a whopping 50 percent of positive things their partners are doing and they see negativity when it's not there. People who give their partner the cold shoulder—deliberately ignoring the partner or responding minimally—damage the relationship by making their partner feel worthless and invisible, as if they're not there, not valued. And people who treat their partners with contempt and criticize them not only kill the love in the relationship, but they also kill their partner's ability to fight off viruses and cancers. Being mean is the death knell of relationships.

Kindness, on the other hand, glues couples together. Research independent from theirs has shown that kindness (along with emotional stability) is the most important predictor of satisfaction and stability in a marriage. Kindness makes each partner feel cared for, understood, and validated—feel loved. "My bounty is as boundless as the sea," says Shakespeare's Juliet. "My love as deep; the more I give to thee, / The more I have, for both are infinite." That's how kindness works too: there's a great deal of evidence showing the more someone receives or witnesses kindness, the more they will be kind themselves, which leads to upward spirals of love and generosity in a relationship.

There are two ways to think about kindness. You can think about it as a fixed trait: either you have it or you don't. Or you could think of kindness as a muscle. In some people, that muscle is naturally stronger than in others, but it can grow stronger in everyone with exercise. Masters tend to think about kindness as a muscle. They know that they have to exercise it to keep it in shape. They know, in other words, that a good relationship requires sustained hard work.

"If your partner expresses a need," explained Julie Gottman, "and you are tired, stressed, or distracted, then the generous spirit comes in when a partner makes a bid, and you still turn toward your partner."

In that moment, the easy response may be to turn away from your partner and focus on your iPad or your book or the television, to mumble "Uh huh" and move on with your life, but neglecting small moments of emotional connection will slowly wear away at your relationship. Neglect creates distance between partners and breeds resentment in the one who is being ignored.

The hardest time to practice kindness is, of course, during a fight—but this is also the most important time to be kind. Letting contempt and aggression spiral out of control during a conflict can inflict irrevocable damage on a relationship.

"Kindness doesn't mean that we don't express our anger," Julie Gottman explained, "but the kindness informs how we choose to express the anger. You can throw spears at your partner. Or you can explain why you're hurt and angry, and that's the kinder path."

John Gottman elaborated on those spears: "Disasters will say things differently in a fight. Disasters will say 'You're late. What's wrong with you? You're just like your mom.' Masters will say 'I feel bad for picking on you about your lateness, and I know it's not your fault, but it's really annoying that you're late again.'"

❖❖❖

For the hundreds of thousands of couples getting married this month—and for the millions of couples currently together, married or not—the lesson from the research is clear: If you want to have a stable, healthy relationship, exercise kindness early and often.

When people think about practicing kindness, they often think about small acts of generosity, like buying each other little gifts or giving one another back rubs every now and then. While those are great examples of generosity, kindness can also be built into the very backbone of a relationship through the way partners interact with each other on a day-to-day basis, whether or not there are back rubs and chocolates involved.

One way to practice kindness is by being generous about your partner's intentions. From the research of the Gottmans, we know that disasters see negativity in their relationship even when it is not there. An angry wife may assume, for example, that when her husband left the toilet seat up, he was deliberately trying to annoy her. But he may have just absent-mindedly forgotten to put the seat down.

Or say a wife is running late to dinner (again), and the husband assumes that she doesn't value him enough to show up to their date on time after he took the trouble to make a reservation and leave work early so that they could spend a romantic evening together. But it turns out that the wife was running late because she stopped by a store to pick him up a gift for their special night out. Imagine her joining him for dinner, excited to deliver her gift, only to realize that he's in a sour mood because he misinterpreted what was motivating her behavior. The ability to interpret your partner's actions and intentions charitably can soften the sharp edge of conflict.

"Even in relationships where people are frustrated, it's almost always the case that there are positive things going on and people trying to do the right thing," psychologist Ty Tashiro told me. "A lot of times, a partner is trying to do the right thing even if it's executed poorly. So appreciate the intent."

Another powerful kindness strategy revolves around shared joy. One of the telltale signs of the disaster couples Gottman studied was their inability to connect over each other's good news. When one person in the relationship shared the good news of, say, a promotion at work with excitement, the other would respond with wooden disinterest by checking his watch or shutting the conversation down with a comment like, "That's nice."

We've all heard that partners should be there for each other when the going gets rough. But research shows that being there for each other when things go *right* is actually more important for relationship quality. How someone responds to a partner's good news can have dramatic consequences for the relationship.

In one study from 2006, psychological researcher Shelly Gable and her colleagues brought young adult couples into the lab to discuss recent positive events from their lives. The psychologists wanted to know how partners would respond to each other's good news. They found that, in general, couples responded to each other's good news in four different ways that they called: *passive destructive*, *active destructive*, *passive constructive*, and *active constructive*.

Let's say that one partner had recently received the excellent news that she got into medical school. She would say something like "I got into my top choice med school!"

Those who showed genuine interest in their partner's joys were more likely to be together.

If her partner responded in a *passive destructive* manner, he would ignore the event. For example, he might say something like: "You wouldn't believe the great news I got yesterday! I won a free t-shirt!"

If her partner responded in a *passive constructive* way, he would acknowledge the good news, but in a half-hearted, understated way. A typical passive constructive response is saying "That's great, babe" as he texts his buddy on his phone.

In the third kind of response, *active destructive*, the partner would diminish the good news his partner just got: "Are you sure you can handle all the studying? And what about the cost? Med school is so expensive!"

Finally, there's *active constructive* responding. If her partner responded in this way, he stopped what he was doing and engaged wholeheartedly with her: "That's great! Congratulations! When did you find out? Did they call you? What classes will you take first semester?"

Among the four response styles, active constructive responding is the kindest. While the other response styles are joy-killers, active constructive responding allows the partner to savor her joy and gives the couple an opportunity to bond over the good news. In the parlance of the Gottmans, active constructive responding is a way of "turning toward" your partners bid (sharing the good news) rather than "turning away" from it.

Active constructive responding is critical for healthy relationships. In the 2006 study, Gable and her colleagues followed up with the couples two months later to see if they were still together. The psychologists found that the only difference between the couples who were together and those who broke up was active constructive responding. Those who showed genuine interest in their partner's joys were more likely to be together. In an earlier study, Gable found that active constructive responding was also associated with higher relationship quality and more intimacy between partners.

There are many reasons why relationships fail, but if you look at what drives the deterioration of many relationships, it's often a breakdown of kindness. As the normal stresses of a life together pile up—with children, career, friends, in-laws, and other distractions crowding out the time for romance and intimacy—couples may put less effort into their relationship and let the petty grievances they hold against one another tear them apart. In most marriages, levels of satisfaction drop dramatically within the first few years together. But among couples who not only endure, but live happily together for years and years, the spirit of kindness and generosity guides them forward.

Kindly Lights

Kindness is more important than wisdom, and the recognition of this is the beginning of wisdom.
—THEODORE ISAAC RUBIN, M.D.

Recompense injury with justice, and recompense kindness with kindness.

—CONFUCIUS

Kindness is the golden chain by which society is bound together.

—GOETHE

If speaking kindly to plants helps them grow, imagine what speaking kindly to humans can do.
—ANONYMOUS

10

My Religion Is Kindness

Richard Rohr

I think the genius of the Dalai Lama and of Buddhism is that they do not get lost in metaphysics and argumentation about dogmas and doctrines. They stay at a different level and thus avoid much of the endless disagreement that we find within Christianity. They do not argue about "what" but spend all of their time on "how"—which we have tended to neglect while we argue about "what." As the Dalai Lama says, "My religion is kindness." We could dismiss that as lightweight theology, until we remember that Jesus said, "This is my commandment: you must love one another" (John 13:34). Kindness is supposed to be the religion of Christians too!

As we continue to mature, we come to a sure sense that there is a deep okayness to life. "All will be well, all will be well, and every manner of things will be well," as Julian of Norwich put it. We can live more and more within unitive consciousness and know the Divine Life itself is flowing through us. Your life is not about you; you are about Life! Life, your life, all life, the one life that we all share, is going somewhere and somewhere good. You do not need to navigate the river, for you are already flowing within it. For some reason, it takes a long time to get where we already are. Our goal is to intentionally participate in this mystery of what has always been our True Self. The Great Ones all agree on this: This one life, this True Self that lasts forever, is Love (1 Corinthians 13:8, 13). And we practice for it by being kind to everyone now.

11

The Tender Gravity of Kindness

Naomi Shihab Nye

Before you know what kindness really is
you must lose things,
feel the future dissolve in a moment
like salt in a weakened broth.
What you held in your hand,
what you counted and carefully saved,
all this must go so you know
how desolate the landscape can be
between the regions of kindness.
How you ride and ride
thinking the bus will never stop,
the passengers eating maize and chicken
will stare out the window forever.
Before you learn the tender gravity of kindness
you must travel where the Indian in a white
        poncho

lies dead by the side of the road.
You must see how this could be you,
how he too was someone
who journeyed through the night with plans
and the simple breath that kept him alive.

Before you know kindness as the deepest thing
      inside,
you must know sorrow as the other deepest
      thing.
You must wake up with sorrow.
You must speak to it till your voice
catches the thread of all sorrows
and you see the size of the cloth.
Then it is only kindness that makes sense any-
      more,
only kindness that ties your shoes
and sends you out into the day to gaze at bread,
only kindness that raises its head
from the crowd of the world to say
It is I you have been looking for,
and then goes with you everywhere
like a shadow or a friend.

12

A Meditation on Lovingkindness

Jack Kornfield

This meditation uses words, images, and feelings to evoke a lovingkindness and friendliness toward oneself and others.

With each recitation of the phrases, we are expressing an intention, planting the seeds of loving wishes over and over in our heart.

With a loving heart as the background, all that we attempt, all that we encounter will open and flow easily.

You can begin the practice of lovingkindness by meditating for fifteen or twenty minutes in a quiet place. Let yourself sit in a comfortable fashion. Let your body rest and be relaxed. Let your heart be soft. Let go of any plans and preoccupations.

Begin with yourself. Breathe gently, and recite inwardly the following traditional phrases directed to your own well-being. You begin with yourself because without loving yourself it is almost impossible to love others.

May I be filled with lovingkindness.
May I be safe from inner and outer dangers.
May I be well in body and mind.
May I be at ease and happy.

As you repeat these phrases, picture yourself as you are now, and hold that image in a heart of lovingkindness. Or perhaps you will find it easier to picture yourself as a young and beloved child. Adjust the words and images in any way you wish. Create the exact phrases that best open your heart of kindness. Repeat these phrases over and over again, letting the feelings permeate your body and mind. Practice this meditation for a number of weeks, until the sense of lovingkindness for yourself grows.

Be aware that this meditation may at times feel mechanical or awkward. It can also bring up feelings contrary to lovingkindness, feelings of irritation and anger. If this happens, it is especially important to be patient and kind toward yourself, allowing whatever arises to be received in a spirit of friendliness and kind affection.

When you feel you have established some stronger sense of lovingkindness for yourself, you can then expand your meditation to include others. After focusing on yourself for five or ten minutes, choose a benefactor, someone in your life who has loved or truly cared for you. Picture this person and carefully recite the same phrases:

May you be filled with lovingkindness.
May you be safe from inner and outer dangers.
May you be well in body and mind.
May you be at ease and happy.

Let the image and feelings you have for your benefactor support the meditation. Whether the image or feelings are clear or not does not matter. In meditation they will be subject to change. Simply continue to plant the seeds of loving wishes, repeating the phrases gently no matter what arises.

Expressing gratitude to our benefactors is a natural form of love. In fact, some people find lovingkindness for themselves so hard, they begin their practice with a benefactor. This too is fine. The rule in lovingkindness practice is to follow the way that most easily opens your heart.

Kindly Lights

Carry out a random act of kindness, with no expectation of reward, safe in the knowledge that one day someone might do the same for you.

—PRINCESS DIANA

Kindness in words creates confidence. Kindness in thinking creates profoundness. Kindness in giving creates love.

—LAO TZU

Hear me, O LORD; for thy lovingkindness is good: turn unto me according to the multitude of thy tender mercies.

—PSALMS 69:16

Look for Unannounced Angels

Joyce Rupp

It seemed to take forever to walk out of Ponferrada. We left the *refugio* when traffic in the city of 50,000 peaked. We had a hard time finding our way through the busy streets. Most intersections were not marked with the usual Camino symbols of the scallop shell or the yellow arrow. Even when the streets were marked, the shells were usually pressed into sidewalk tiles instead of on the sides of buildings, making it difficult to detect the shells. To add to our frustration, it began to rain. As we moved along the street, we grew anxious because we had not seen a marker in quite some time. We looked up at the buildings, down on the sidewalk and all around for signs. To our relief, we spotted another shell imprinted on the sidewalk ahead of us.

We took about fifteen steps forward when I heard a rough voice behind me say, "This way." A blond-bearded man in a long, flowing, red rain cape motioned toward an alley to the right. On the wall of the alley, I noticed a yellow arrow pointing in that direction. Seeing it, I called to Tom but he missed seeing the arrow and hesitated following. I urged him to come. Then we both quickly turned and followed the silent pilgrim who was already moving rapidly down steep steps toward a park-like area along a wide river.

The tall man's cape blew in the windy rain and he reached out to wrap it closer around himself. He appeared mysterious, a bit sinister almost, as he hurried through the alley and down the steps with his head slightly bowed. I wondered about the wisdom of our decision to follow him on the route. Perhaps it was a ruse to lure pilgrims away for robbery. Several times others, like the French pilgrims, warned us to be wary of those who might want to rob us when we walked through larger cities like Ponferrada.

About the time fear flooded over me, I noticed he was taking us on an alternative path leading along a beautiful waterway lined with trees, a much more pleasant walk than through the busy industrial streets we left behind. His angular body and thin, long legs helped him move swiftly. We almost ran to keep up. We feared if we lost him, we might easily lose the direction of the path because there were few arrows on this route, as well. When we lagged far behind, he slowed his pace, and we were able to keep him in view. The red-caped man looked back once or twice to see if we were following. This pattern of his slowing down and our speeding up continued some forty minutes until we reached the edge of the city where it was obvious the central path lay ahead. Then the silent pilgrim picked up his pace and soon was nowhere to be seen.

Like the two on the road to Emmaus, Tom and I pondered that unusual event. How was it, we marveled as we walked along, that the stranger came by just at the moment of our need? How kind that he called out for us to follow him. What caused him to slow his pace so we could keep up with him? Why did he care enough about us to even bother to show us the alternative route? We both felt a certain mystical aura about the experience, almost as if the man was an angel sent to make our journey easier.

By mid-morning we finally found a place where we could stop for coffee. The rain continued so we took off our wet backpacks and left them outside the front entrance. We stepped inside and to our surprise we saw our "angel." We went over to him and thanked him for his kindness. One of us mentioned how grateful we were that he slowed his pace for us. At this he laughed uneasily and muttered, "Don't read more into this than it is." He followed this by saying it was only his mood that led him to walk slowly.

His comment broke the mystical spell, but I still felt some divine intervention had blessed us. Although the tall man did not believe he was an instrument of God's goodness that day, we certainly did. This incident led me to think about how this sort of experience is actually more common than is supposed. People may not deliberately intend to be an instrument of God but they often are, without their realizing it.

The first time this happened on the journey we were en route to Spain. Because of weather conditions we arrived late into the Newark airport, causing us to miss our overnight flight to Madrid. It was 10:30 p.m. and we had not eaten dinner. We stood at the airline counter trying to understand the complicated directions for getting to our lodging for the night. The ticket agent looked exhausted and there was still a long line of passengers behind us to be reticketed. We jotted down the directions as quickly as possible so we wouldn't increase their waiting. Then we started down the concourse.

Neither of us had a clue as to where we were headed. A porter passed by us, noticed our confused looks, and asked if he could help us out. After a few moments of trying to explain, he said, "Here, follow me" and proceeded to walk with us for ten minutes to an elevator that took us in the right direction. As I turned around to say "thanks," he was already on his way, disappearing around the corner. In that moment, I had a strong sense we would be taken care of on the Camino. Even though I had fears and misgivings in the weeks ahead, I was quietly reassured that night because of this angel-like encounter.

While our red-caped angel appeared mysteriously and helped us out physically, another angel on the Camino surprised me by touching my heart. There were three times when I cried on the pilgrimage. The first time occurred when I experienced a hospitaler at the refugio in Tosantos. This refugio was one of the most welcoming places on the Camino. Much of this was due to his presence. He was a genuine hospitaler, a robust Spaniard who laughed and smiled as he invited weary travelers in, often extending a warm hug with his greeting. His real name was José; but Tom and I always referred to him as Señor Cantante (Mr. Singer) because he was full of music.

After most of us arrived in the late afternoon Señor Cantante invited pilgrims to join him in practicing songs for the evening prayer. We practiced several chants and the refrain to a great peregrino (pilgrim) song. His enthusiasm proved contagious. His brown eyes lit up as he introduced various melodies and affirmed our ability to sing the chants beautifully. As he directed us to soften the notes and keep the tempo, he sometimes closed his eyes in such a satisfying manner he looked like he was about to levitate. His sincere warmth easily permeated those of us present.

This enthusiasm extended into the dinner hour. Señor Cantante not only led the singing but he also helped to prepare and serve a massive pot of spaghetti with some carrots in it. An equally huge plastic mixing bowl of greens followed and then pieces of fresh fruit for dessert. He even passed a roll of toilet paper around the table when there were no napkins to be found! The conversation among the thirty or so of us that night rang out with both laughter and meaningful sharing. Much of it was due to the atmosphere Señor Cantante engendered.

After the meal we went up to the third floor where, of all surprises, we discovered a little prayer room off to the side with a tiny door through which we entered. I felt like Alice in Wonderland. The room had old round logs on the ceiling, a thin, tan rug on the floor, and cereal bowls holding semi-wilted geranium blossoms in front of a faded hearth. We sat in a circle although there was barely room for all of us. Señor Cantante led us through the same prayer service as at the previous place, only we sang all the refrains plus the pilgrim song he taught us. I was thrilled to be singing, to have some music, because I had missed music so much. Even though my body was dead tired, my heart soared.

I am not sure exactly what this kind hospitaler triggered in my emotional response the next morning. We had been on the road for eleven days and maybe I just needed some attentive comfort and care. I only know that when we prepared to leave, Señor Cantante stood at the door to send us off. I thanked him for his hospitality and he responded by telling me it was a pleasure to do so for people like us. He then reached toward me, cupped my face gently in his hands, kissed me on either cheek, and blessed me with the farewell of "Buen Camino." An unmistakable touch of divine love filled that gesture. I sensed the power of a very special soul touching mine. Tears welled up and fell upon my cheeks. I looked to see that Tom was crying, too. My voice wavered as I bid Señor Cantante fare-well in that poignant moment.

As I look back on our Camino days, many unan-nounced angels came into our lives at just the right time to help us with their considerate care: store clerks, refugio directors and volunteers, waiters and waitresses, farmers and city folk, and, of course, all those pilgrims who stepped forth when we needed them most. As I look back in reflection on what hap-pened with our many "angels," I realize how fortunate we were to have someone there for us at the exact moment we needed them.

Since my return from the Camino, others have told me about strangers who offered them solace in a hospital emergency room, unknown people who stopped to help change a flat tire, unnamed persons who reached out to extend help or gave information at precisely the time of greatest need. These anonymous people rarely stayed for very long but their good deeds are tucked away in the hearts of those they assisted.

I have often wondered if people like the red-caped man, Señor Cantante, or the elderly woman knew how much their kindness mirrored divine benevolence. I doubt they did. I doubt that any of us are normally aware of having a profound effect on another unless someone tells us about it. We may do a good deed but unless the events are startling or unusual, they generally fade into life's experience without much of a second thought.

Yet, the slightest of actions may have a great influence on another. Each of us can be an angel in some way if we take the dictionary definition of angel as our source of description: a messenger, a spirit or a spiritual being employed by God to communicate with humankind. And what do these angels communicate? For us on the Camino, they brought the message of God's compassion, kindness, thoughtfulness, and solace. We learned these angels are everywhere if the eyes of our souls are vigilant enough to notice.

The Camino helped me believe in the unique way God moves in our lives through the presence of other human beings who show up at the right time. Even when these strangers are oblivious to how they are an instrument of good, they act in a manner surprisingly beneficial and helpful. We never know when someone we meet might be just the right person we need for the moment. We rarely expect unannounced angels in our midst but, oh, how wonderful they are when they show up to grace us with their gifts.

14

I Had Lunch with God

Joseph G. Healey

A little East African boy in Dar es Salaam wanted to meet God. He knew that it was a long trip to where God lived, so he packed his bag with small, sweet cakes and a large bottle of soda and started on his journey.

He had been on his way for about ten minutes when he met an old woman. She was sitting in a park by the Indian Ocean just staring at some African birds. The boy sat down next to her and opened his bag. He was about to take a drink from his soda when he noticed that the old lady looked hungry, so he offered her a small cake. She gratefully accepted it and smiled at him. Her smile was so pretty that the boy wanted to see it again. So he offered her a drink from his soda. Again she smiled at him. The boy was delighted!

The little East African boy and the old woman sat there all afternoon eating and drinking and smiling, but they never said a word. As it grew dark, the boy realized how tired he was and got up to leave. But before he had gone more than a few steps he turned around, ran back to the old woman, and gave her a big hug. She gave him her biggest smile.

When the boy opened the door to his own home a short time later, his mother was surprised by the look of joy on his face.

She asked him, "What did you do today that makes you so happy?"

He replied, "I had lunch with God." But before his mother could respond, he added, "You know what? She's got the most beautiful smile I've ever seen!"

Meanwhile, the old woman, also radiant with joy, returned to her home in the Upanga section of town.

Her son was stunned by the look of peace on her face and he asked, "Mother, what did you do today that makes you so happy?"

She replied, "I ate small cakes and drank soda in the park with God." And then, before her son could respond, she added, "You know, he's much younger than I expected."

15

In Praise of the Crushed Heart

Dorothy Day

Here is a letter we received today: "I took a gentleman seemingly in need of spiritual and temporal guidance into my home on a Sunday afternoon. Let him have a nap on my bed, went through the want ads with him, made coffee and sandwiches for him, and when he left, I found my wallet had gone also."

I can only say that the saints would only bow their heads and not try to understand or judge. They received no thanks—well, then, God had to repay them. They forbore to judge, and it was as though they took off their cloak besides their coat to give away. This is expecting heroic charity, of course. But these things happen for our discouragement, for our testing. We are sowing the seed of love, and we are not living in the harvest time. We must love to the point of folly, and we are indeed fools, as Our Lord Himself was who died for such a one as this. We lay down our lives, too, when we have performed so painfully thankless an act, for our correspondent is poor in this world's goods. It is agony to go through such bitter experiences, because we all want to love, we desire with a great longing to love our fellows, and our hearts are often crushed at such rejections. But, as a Carmelite nun said to me last week, "It is the crushed heart which is the soft heart, the tender heart."

Kindly Lights

Kind words can be short and easy to speak,
but their echoes are truly endless.

—MOTHER TERESA

Ask yourself: Have you been kind today? Make
kindness your daily modus operandi and change
your world.

—ANNIE LENNOX

Wherever there is a human being, there is a chance
for kindness.

—SENECA

16

A Path Toward Sainthood

Pope Francis

Dear Brothers and Sisters, good morning,

We are beginning to understand that all Christians, insofar as they have been baptized, are equal in dignity before the Lord and share in the same vocation, that is, to sainthood (cf. *Lumen Gentium*, nn. 39–42). Now let us ask ourselves: what does this universal vocation to being saints consist in? And how can we realize it?

1. First of all, we must bear clearly in mind that sanctity is not something we can procure for ourselves, that we can obtain by our own qualities and abilities. Sanctity is a gift, it is a gift granted to us by the Lord Jesus, when He takes us to Himself and clothes us in Himself, He makes us like Him. In his Letter to the Ephesians, the Apostle Paul states that "Christ loved the church and gave himself up for her,

that he might sanctify her" (5:25–26). You see, saint-hood truly is the most beautiful face of the Church, the most beautiful face: it is to rediscover oneself in communion with God, in the fullness of his life and of his love. Sanctity is understood, then, not as a pre-rogative of the few: sanctity is a gift offered to all, no one excluded, by which the distinctive character of every Christian is constituted.

2. All this makes us understand that, in order to be saints, there is no need to be bishops, priests or reli-gious: no, we are all called to be saints! So, many times we are tempted to think that sainthood is reserved only to those who have the opportunity to break away from daily affairs in order to dedicate themselves exclusively to prayer. But it is not so! Some think that sanctity is to close your eyes and to look like a holy icon. No! This is not sanctity! Sanctity is some-thing greater, deeper, which God gives us. Indeed, it is precisely in living with love and offering one's own Christian witness in everyday affairs that we are called to become saints. And each in the conditions and the state of life in which he or she finds him- or herself. But you are consecrated. Are you consecrat-ed? —Be a saint by living out your donation and your ministry with joy. Are you married? —Be a saint by

loving and taking care of your husband or your wife, as Christ did for the Church. Are you an unmarried baptized person? —Be a saint by carrying out your work with honesty and competence and by offering time in the service of your brothers and sisters. "But, father, I work in a factory; I work as an accountant, only with numbers; you can't be a saint there. . . ." "Yes, yes you can! There, where you work, you can become a saint. God gives you the grace to become holy. God communicates himself to you." Always, in every place, one can become a saint, that is, one can open oneself up to this grace, which works inside us and leads us to holiness. Are you a parent or a grandparent? —Be a saint by passionately teaching your children or grandchildren to know and to follow Jesus. And it takes so much patience to do this: to be a good parent, a good grandfather, a good mother, a good grandmother; it takes so much patience and with this patience comes holiness: by exercising patience. Are you a catechist, an educator or a volunteer?—Be a saint by becoming a visible sign of God's love and of his presence alongside us. This is it: every state of life leads to holiness, always! In your home, on the street, at work, at church, in that moment and in your state of life, the path to sainthood has been opened. Don't be discouraged to pursue this path. It is God alone who gives us the grace. The Lord asks only this: that we be in communion with Him and at the service of our brothers and sisters.

3. At this point, each one of us can make a little examination of conscience; we can do it right now, each one respond to himself, in silence: how have we responded up to now to the Lord's call to sanctity? Do I want to become a little better, a little more Christian? This is the path to holiness. When the Lord invites us to become saints, he doesn't call us to something heavy, sad . . . quite the contrary! It's an invitation to share in his joy, to live and to offer with joy every moment of our life, by making it become at the same time a gift of love for the people around us. If we understand this, everything changes and takes on new meaning, a beautiful meaning, a meaning that begins with little everyday things. For example: a lady goes to the market to buy groceries and finds a neighbor there, so they begin to talk and then they come to gossiping and this lady says: "No, no, no, I won't speak badly about anyone." This is a step towards sainthood, it helps you become more holy. Then, at home, your son wants to talk a little about his ideas: "Oh, I am so tired, I worked so hard today. . . ." — "But you sit

down and listen to your son, who needs it!" And you sit down, you listen to him patiently: this is a step towards sainthood. Then the day ends, we are all tired, but there are the prayers. We say our prayers: this too is a step towards holiness. Then comes Sunday and we go to Mass, we take communion, sometimes preceded by a beautiful confession which cleans us a little. This is a step towards sainthood. Then we think of Our Lady, so good, so beautiful, and we take up the rosary and we pray it. This is a step towards sainthood. Then I go out to the street, I see a poor person in need, I stop and address him, I give him something: it is a step towards sainthood. These are little things, but many little steps to sanctity. Every step towards sainthood makes us better people, free from selfishness and being closed within ourselves, and opens us to our brothers and sisters and to their needs.

Dear friends, in the First Letter of St. Peter this is asked of us: "As each has received a gift, employ it for one another, as good stewards of God's varied grace: whoever speaks, as one who utters oracles of God; whoever renders service, as one who renders it by the strength which God supplies; in order that in everything God may be glorified through Jesus Christ" (4:10–11). This is the invitation to holiness! Let us accept it with joy, and let us support one another, for the path to sainthood is not taken alone, each one for oneself, but is traveled together, in that one body that is the Church, loved and made holy by the Lord Jesus Christ. Let us go forward with courage on this path to holiness.

17

Building a Bridge with Kind Words

Terry Golway

There were lots of unfamiliar faces at Mass that morning, visitors invited to share the day with their friends from the parish. Some of them were not Catholic, though that was hardly a surprise. In my part of the country, the polyglot Northeast, such family-church celebrations rarely are for Catholics only. Intermarriage, ecumenism, secular education and new career paths have brought Catholics, Jews and Protestants together in ways unimaginable a generation ago. I've been to bar mitzvahs and a bris or two in recent years; my Jewish and Protestant friends came to my wedding and the baptisms of my two children. We are no longer strangers as we were as recently as the 1960s.

The Gospel read at my daughter's first Communion Mass a year ago was, as is the custom on the

Sunday after Easter, the doubting Thomas passage from John. It is one of my favorites, for who among us cannot sympathize with Thomas? Who among us has never had doubts?

I found myself cringing, however, as the passage's opening words echoed through the church. John describes how the heartbroken disciples, grieving the loss of Jesus, were gathered together and in hiding for fear of the Jews.

I knew that several of the children making first Communion were the products of Catholic–Jewish marriages, and I knew that their Jewish relatives were in the pews, some of them first-time visitors to a Catholic church. They were upset when they heard those words, and I think understandably so. A Jewish relative of one of the first communicants said she had never heard a bad reference to Christians in her synagogue, but during her first visit to a Catholic church, she heard a description of Christ's disciples in hiding for fear of the Jews. Obviously, the Gospel is the Gospel, and I'm not suggesting for a moment that we ought to rewrite the words of John, Luke, Mark and Matthew to accommodate modern sensibilities. (As an aside, I was startled a number of years ago at the new translation of Luke's poetic story of Christ's birth, which told us that there was no room for Mary and Joseph in the place where travelers lodged. That had all the poetry and music of a government white paper. It was good to get back our beloved old inn when the new translation was replaced by still another revision.) Obviously, there were real, historical reasons why the disciples were in hiding and in fear of their lives.

Nevertheless, we should remember when this Gospel is read. It is not only the Sunday after Easter, but also, in many dioceses, the Sunday of first Communion. And that means, in areas like the Northeast, it's likely that Jew—friends, relatives, and even parents of the first communicants are in the church. Surely it would not take away from the occasion if a homilist briefly and lovingly put John's words in context, if only to point out that the disciples were Jews themselves, or that, as we know from the Creed, Christ suffered under Pontius Pilate, who was not a Pharisee but a servant of the Roman Empire. The men who scourged and mocked him were Roman soldiers, not Jews. This may (or should) be self-evident to most of us, but it might bear repeating on such occasions.

This year, my family helped celebrate the first Communion of a neighbor on the second Sunday after Easter (in our parish, families have a choice between the first two Sundays after Easter). The Gospel, of course, was different, but the dynamics were the same: My neighbors had invited Jewish friends to the Mass, and there were several Jewish relatives of other communicants in the church. My pastor, who would be embarrassed if I told you his name is Monsignor John Doran, noticed several young boys wearing yarmulkes in the pews just before Mass began. As I later learned, he stopped and chatted for a moment with the boys' parents.

A few minutes later, as my pastor began his homily, he delivered a special greeting to the Jewish family he had noticed. (There were several other Jewish families in the pews, mutual friends of my neighbor.) Recalling the words of Pope John Paul II, he reminded us that Jews are our spiritual elders who gave to us the knowledge of the one true God. He said he hoped they would feel as welcome in our church as we have felt when welcomed in the local synagogue.

It was a lovely and profoundly spiritual moment. I talked with the father of those boys at my neighbor's first Communion party. He was visibly touched to be greeted in such a special and affectionate way, on such an occasion. When the priest approached me,

I didn't know what he was going to say, the boys' father told me. I thought maybe we were in trouble. He laughed when he said this, but it was clear that there had been, in fact, a moment of discomfort, one that many of us can understand. He was, after all, inside an unfamiliar house of worship with mysterious rituals and protocol, and suddenly he's approached by the resident clergyman. I certainly would have suspected trouble! (Did I do something wrong? Am I dressed inappropriately?) But there was no trouble at all; quite the opposite.

For my part, I was proud to see a bridge built with nothing more, and nothing less, than kind words.

18

People Will Always Be Kind

Michael Leach

I pick up Vickie from Adult Day Care and drive to Chipotle for takeout. We park in the handicapped space in front. A young African American in an apron rushes out the door and holds it open for us. "Mister, I want to show you something," he says. "I have a son!"

"That's wonderful, Andre!"

Andre escorts us to the counter and runs to the back for his cellphone.

Molly with the Smiling Blue Eyes stands over the food. "Let me guess," she says. "White rice, pinto beans, chicken, just a little hot sauce on both."

"I'm proud of you, Molly. Your mom must be very proud."

She loads up both plates. Vickie squeezes herself against my back, her arms wrapped around my chest, her head resting on my back like a child as we toddle alongside the counter. This sight kills people. They can't take it. They want to feed us.

Jeter, as in Derek Jeter (that's what I call him because he's a Yankee fan), is at the cash register. We talk about the World Series. Molly passes over the bag, and I hand him a twenty. "No charge," Jeter says.

The manager Justin, who knows every customer, started comping us about six months ago. Not every time or even a lot of times but enough times to make me wonder if my old man pants (baggy blue with a drawstring) and the same old Cubs T-shirt makes me look rundown. Jeter says it's policy not to charge good customers every now and then, but frankly, I think it's the Mike and Vickie Shuffle. Certainly kindness shines through their gesture in choosing us.

And it's not just Chipotle people who are kind to us.

Abdul at Boston Chicken sometimes gives us two platters of turkey for the price of one and always slips a free slice of apple pie in the bag.

Michael, the manager of Bull's Head Diner in Stamford, likes to stuff a free brownie the size of a brick into our bag. Gabriel the archangel, a waiter who has been at the diner since we started going there twenty years ago, carries our bag to the car and opens the door for Vickie and always asks about our grand-kids, and we ask him about his family, and his mother in Mexico has made it through the earthquake you'll be happy to know.

The Dalai Lama once counseled followers to be kind whenever and however possible. "And it is always possible," he added.

"Don't go yet!" Andre catches up to us before we leave Chipotle. "Look," he says and hands me his cell phone.

"He's beautiful!" I say. "Look at those chubby cheeks! What's his name?"

"Amir."

"A great name. You have other kids?"

"My first son, his name is Andre like me. He's four."

"I remember when our grandkids were four. That's a fun age. I'm putting you and Li'l Andre and Amir in my prayers, right up here where I pray all the time."

"Thank you. I am praying for you."

I wave at the kids behind the counter. "Thanks, guys!"

The Chiptoleans wave, even the ones chopping pork and slicing steak and boiling rice that steams up into their faces like heady incense.

We pull into our driveway. A white plastic bag hangs on the doorknob. Fresh tomatoes, big ones, little ones, some as red as the Chipotle logo, others yellow as custard. No note. Just the tomatoes. Sometimes I think people are conspiring to feed us.

I suspect the Tomato Fairy is Terry Kutzen, one of Vickie's golfing pals from the old days who stays in touch. Whenever it's suppertime, and I don't know what to get, Terry calls up out of the blue and says, "I just made meat loaf and got plenty left. It's hot and ready to go. Can I come over?" If it's not her meat loaf, it's her chicken with herbs and spices from the Far East, or plastic containers of magical chicken soup that could cure lower back pain, and it's always enough for three full meals.

The Tomato Fairy also could have been Darlene from around the corner whose husband had Alzheimer's, too, and died three years ago, and who bakes more varieties of cookies than Famous Amos. Or maybe it's Helen from down the block who appears bearing cellophane wrapped platters with a three course gourmet meal every now and then or, better yet, a paper plate overflowing with lip-burning chocolate chippers just out of the oven. Or it could be Sibley next door who calls and says, "I just tried something new. Would you like to try it?" Before she moved to Florida it was Jane, who specialized in roast beef that would slice itself as your eyes slobbered over it. And it's always our son Chris's great big heart of a girlfriend Jessica who cooks all day dinners for our whole family, on Thanksgiving and Christmas and any old Sunday at all, at our house or theirs, and even takes the lead in cleaning the dishes. I tell you: people will always be kind. Vickie and I can afford to eat at our diner every night but nothing tastes as good as the kindness that carries our bag to the car or opens the door for us at Chipotle or hangs a plastic bag of just picked tomatoes on our doorknob.

Yes, it's a big bad world out there but after every earthquake we watch men and women clawing through rocks to save children, for every hurricane we see neighbors helping neighbors and strangers in other lands sending cans of food through their churches, and for every Las Vegas or Sandy Hook we behold people standing in line at hospitals to donate precious blood. And for every klutz like me who cares for a Vickie and can only cook Campbell's Soup, there are always, always, Tomato Fairies.

19

Practice Kindness All Day to Everybody

Jack Kerouac

The world you see is just a movie in your mind.
Rocks don't see it.
Bless and sit down.
Forgive and forget.
Practice kindness all day to everybody
and you will realize you're already
in heaven now.
That's the story.
That's the message.
Nobody understands it,
nobody listens, they're
all running around like chickens with heads cut
off. I will try to teach it but it will
be in vain, s'why I'll
end up in a shack

praying and being
cool and singing
by my woodstove
making pancakes.

Kindly Lights

Be kind whenever possible; and it is always possible.

—Tenzin Gyatso, the 14th Dalai Lama

I expect to pass through this world but once. Any good therefore that I can do or any kindness that I can show for any fellow creature, let me do it now. Let me not defer or neglect it, for I shall not pass this way again.

—Ralph Waldo Emerson

Make it a practice to judge persons and things in the most favorable light at all times and under all circumstances.

—Saint Vincent de Paul

20

Don't Be a Jerk

James Martin, SJ

"Coarsened" is a word you've probably heard more and more frequently in the past few years. It's most often applied to the state of public discourse in our country, particularly in the political sphere.

Lately, some of our political candidates have been calling one another names, using schoolyard taunts and shouting over one another during televised debates. There have even been articles written that used insights from child psychologists to aid parents hoping to teach their children that this is not how adults should behave. On top of that, your social media feeds (Facebook, Twitter and the like) may be filled with increasing levels of invective. Even in our own church many Catholics seem ready to call another person a "bad Catholic" at the drop of a biretta.

You can be excused for feeling that having a conversation on a controversial topic might prove dangerous for your emotional, psychological, spiritual and maybe even physical health. You might get slugged.

All this reminds me of some great advice I once heard from the Jesuit historian John W. O'Malley, author of several books, including *The First Jesuits* and *What Happened at Vatican II?* But it isn't an aperçu from St. Ignatius Loyola or one of the early Jesuits. Rather, this wisdom came from an older Jesuit whom John had once known. They were three rules for getting along in Jesuit community: (1) You're not God; (2) This isn't heaven; (3) Don't be a jerk. That last one was originally in saltier language—using a synonym for a kind of donkey—but it still works.

The first two are essential for life in general. "You're not God" has multiple implications. First, you can't change most things, so stop trying. Second, you're not in charge, so stop acting as if you were. And third, you don't know everything, so stop acting as if you do. It brings calm, perspective and humility.

The second dictum, "This isn't heaven" can help to reduce the complaining you do. For example, if you live in a Jesuit community where the roof leaks (as ours once did, in my room, for several months) or where the elevator apparently runs up and down on a stream of molasses (as ours has always done), you are reminded to complain less because, well, this isn't heaven.

But it's that last apothegm that I wish more people remembered when they enter into public discussions: "Don't be a jerk." Now, I'm the first to admit that I break that rule from time to time (probably more than I know, since I may not notice it). But today a surprising number of people think nothing of attacking people anonymously on Twitter, calling fellow politicians terrible names and maligning their integrity during debates, posting mean comments on Facebook and shouting over one another on talk shows—basically, being a jerk. And jerkiness is contagious, I think. Seeing public figures shouting on television probably encourages people to do it in their private lives. At the very least, it does not encourage charitable behavior.

How does one avoid that contagion? Here's where some other traditional bits of wisdom can help. First, always give people the benefit of the doubt. Believe it or not, St. Ignatius placed that simple maxim at the beginning of his Spiritual Exercises, where he called it a "Presupposition." "Every good Christian," he wrote, "ought to be more eager to put a good interpretation on a neighbor's statement than to condemn it." Amen.

Second, avoid ad hominem arguments—that is, attacks on the person. The difference here is between "I think your argument is incorrect because…" and "You're a bad Catholic." Avoiding that will ratchet down emotion significantly and help all interactions go more smoothly.

Finally, an overtly spiritual approach: Ask God to help you see others the way God sees them. The old adage that everyone is fighting a battle (or carrying a cross) is helpful. In the Spiritual Exercises, St. Ignatius invites us to imagine the Trinity looking down on all of humanity with love. The next time you're angry with someone, think of the Trinity gazing down on the person you're about to flame.

None of this should prevent people from discussing things, whether one-on-one, online, in public, on television, even on debate nights. You can always disagree. You can even disagree vehemently.

Just don't be a jerk.

21

Stuck in Gander

Michael Schulman

On September 11, 2001, seven thousand passengers were stranded in the tiny town of Gander. Its mayor recently attended "Come from Away," a musical inspired by Gander's hospitality.

The town of Gander, Newfoundland, has six traffic lights and a population of less than thirteen thousand. Snowmobiling is popular, and people leave their car doors unlocked while they're at the grocery store. Its distinguishing feature—and the reason it exists—is its airport, which opened in 1938 and was once the largest in the world, making Gander a crucial transatlantic refuelling stop in the days before long-range jet travel. On September 11, 2001, after flights were rerouted to their nearest airports, thirty-eight jets suddenly landed in Gander, stranding some seven thousand passengers for up to five days in a town with only five hundred hotel rooms.

"The first thing I did was declare a state of emergency," Claude Elliott, the Mayor of Gander since 1996, recalled the other day. A stout sixty-seven-year-old with salt-and-pepper eyebrows and a thick Newfoundland accent, Elliott was in New York with his wife and daughter for the opening of "Come from Away," a new Broadway musical recounting Gander's act of extreme hospitality. It was his third time in New York City. "Going out for breakfast, we were standing on the street corner and I told my wife, 'There's more people here this morning than what live in Gander,'" he said.

Elliott's mayoral duties typically include welcoming conventiongoers and negotiating local disputes, such as the school-bus drivers' strike that was in effect on 9/11. The arrival of the plane people, as the locals called them, nearly doubled the town's population. "I didn't go home for five days," Elliott, who is retiring as mayor in September, recalled. Elementary schools were converted into makeshift dormitories. Volunteers from the Salvation Army and the Red Cross made lunches, and the hockey rink became a walk-in refrigerator. Other logistical problems were trickier. "We ran out of underwear," Elliott said, so more was trucked in from St. John's, two hundred and seven miles away. The plane people hailed from ninety-five countries, including Zimbabwe; kosher meals were required, as was a place for Muslim passengers to pray. A town veterinarian took care of the animals in the planes' cargo holds, including two chimpanzees en route to the Columbus, Ohio, zoo. "A few years later, I got a letter from the Columbus Zoo and a picture of a baby chimpanzee, and they'd named it Gander," Elliott said.

By Day Two of the crisis, Elliott was at the Royal Canadian Legion Hall, initiating marooned passengers as honorary Newfoundlanders, in a ritual named "screeching in": visitors wear yellow sou'westers, eat hard bread and pickled bologna, kiss a cod on the lips, then drink the local rum, called screech, while onlookers bang an "ugly stick" covered in beer-bottle caps. "We started off with seven thousand strangers," Elliott said, "but we finished with seven thousand family members."

In New York, the Mayor, wearing a tuxedo, reappeared in his hotel lobby in Times Square, along with fifteen other Newfoundlanders who had come down for opening night, including a town constable named

Oswald Fudge. They had heard that Cindy Crawford was at the Saturday matinée. "She said she cried, she laughed, but it was the human kindness that really touched her," Elliott said.

The group walked to the Schoenfeld Theatre, while Elliott led them in a Newfoundland ditty called "Aunt Martha's Sheep." Outside the entrance was a press line, including reporters from *Playbill* and the Broadway World website. Elliott went straight for the Canadian press, including camera crews from the local CBC branch and Newfoundland's NTV.

"How does it feel today to be here on the red carpet?" an NTV reporter asked him.

"Like being a kid in a candy store!" Elliott said. "There are very friendly people here. People are waving to you, they say hello to you—almost the same as we do in Newfoundland."

He accompanied his family inside and sat in front of Beverley Bass, who was the first female captain at American Airlines and one of the pilots grounded in 2001. After the show, the actors invited their real-life counterparts onstage for a bow. "Something else to take off my bucket list," Elliott said. Walking out of the theatre, he told an N.Y.P.D. officer, "God bless you for your service," before leading the Ganderites onto a shuttle bus. On their way to the after-party, where screech cocktails and cod awaited, they broke into song again: "There's no place I would rather be than here in Newfoundland!"

"If we were onstage when they were doing the screeching, it would be the real stuff!" Elliott bellowed. The Newfoundlanders cheered.

"And the bottle of screech wouldn't be only half-empty!" someone behind him yelled.

Three days later, the Mayor went back to watch the show alongside the Canadian Prime Minister, Justin Trudeau, who had brought Ivanka Trump. Right before the lights went down, Elliott took a selfie with Trump. "I invited her to Gander," he said afterward. "And if she wants to become an honorary Newfoundlander, we will screech her in.

22

Love Is for Living

Carlo Carretto

Having convinced myself of the primacy of charity, having become aware that in touching charity I am touching God, that in living charity I am living God in me, I must this evening, before finishing my meditation, look at tomorrow to subject it to this light and live it out under the inspiration of this synthesis of love. Basically I must do what Jesus—who brought God's love to earth and communicated it to us— would do in my position. I must remember that the opportunities I shall have to suffer, to pardon, to accept are treasures not to be lost through distraction and values that I must make my own as a worthy response to God's plan in creation.

My life is worth living if I can learn to transform everything that happens to me into love, in imitation of Jesus: because love is for living.

When I meet a brother of mine who has caused me great pain in the past by viciously calumniating me, I shall love him, and in loving him I shall transform the evil done to me into good: because love is for living.

When I have to live with people who do not see things the same way I see them, who say they are enemies of my faith, I shall love them, and in loving them I shall sow the seeds of future dialogue in my heart and theirs: because love is for living.

When I go into a shop to buy something for myself—clothes, food, or whatever it may be—I shall think of my brothers and sisters who are poorer than I am, of the hungry and the naked, and I shall use this thought to govern my purchases, trying out of love to be tight with myself and generous with them: because love is for living.

When I see time's destructive traces in my body and the approach of old age, I shall try to love even more in order to transform the coldest season of life into a total gift of myself in preparation for the imminent holocaust: because love is for living.

When I see the evening of my life, or, on the pavement in a car accident, in the agony of a fatal illness, in the ward of a geriatric hospital, feel the end coming, I shall reach out again for love, striving to accept in joy whatever fate God has had in store for me: because love is for living.

Yes, love is God in me, and if I am in love I am in God, that is, in life, in grace: a sharer in God's being. . . .

If charity is God in me, why look for God any further than myself?

And if God is in me as love, why do I change or disfigure God's face with acts or values which are not love?

23

A Sunday in Purgatory

Henry Morgenthau III

A voluntary inmate immured
in a last resort for seniors,
there are constant reminders
that go with the territory.
The reaper is lurking around that corner.
I am at home, very much at home,
here at Ingleside at Rock Creek,
Distant three miles from my caring daughter
and her family in Cleveland Park.

At Ingleside, a faith-based community
for vintage Presbyterians, I am an old Jew.
But that's another story.
I'm not complaining with so much I want to do,
doing it at my pace, slowly.
Anticipation of death is simply like looking for a new job.

Then suddenly on a Sunday,
talking recklessly while eating brunch,
a gristly piece of meat lodges in my throat.
I struggle for breath, too annoyed to be scared.
Someone pounds my back to no avail.
Out of nowhere, an alert pint-sized waiter
performs the Heimlich maneuver.
I don't believe it will work.
It does! Uncorked, I am freed.

Looking up I see the concerned visage and
reversed collar of a retired Navy chaplain,
pinch hitting as God's messenger for the day.
Had he come to perform the last rites,
to ease my passage from this world to the hereafter?
Don't jump to dark conclusions.
In World War II on active duty,
he learned the Heimlich as well as the *himmlisch*.
Knowing it is best administered
to a standing victim,
he rushed to intervene.
On this day I am twice blessed
with the kindness of strangers.

24

Becoming Kind

Henri Nouwen

Kindness is a beautiful human attribute. When we say, "She is a kind person" or "He surely was kind to me," we express a very warm feeling. In our competitive and often violent world, kindness is not the most frequent response. But when we encounter it we know that we are blessed. Is it possible to grow in kindness, to become a kind person? Yes, but it requires discipline. To be kind means to treat another person as your "kin," your intimate relative. We say, "We are kin" or "He is next of kin." To be kind is to reach out to someone as being of "kindred" spirit.

Here is the great challenge: All people, whatever their color, religion, or sex, belong to humankind and are called to be kind to one another, treating one another as brothers and sisters.

There is hardly a day in our lives in which we are not called to this.

Kindly Light

I have my critics, obviously, but since we're here in Hollywood, I want to think about something that the late, great Chicago film critic, Robert [Roger] Ebert said—and I was fortunate to get to know Roger Ebert and was always inspired by how he handled some really tough stuff.

"Kindness," he wrote, "covers all of my political beliefs."

And when I think about what I'm fighting for, what gets me up every single day, that captures it just about as much as anything. Kindness; empathy—that sense that I have a stake in your success; that I'm going to make sure, just because Malia and Sasha are doing well, that's not enough—I want your kids to do well also. And

I'm willing to help to build good schools so that they get a great education, even if mine are already getting a great education.

—PRESIDENT BARACK OBAMA

25

Ten Commandments of Kindness

James H. Kroeger, MM

Poets and philosophers, sages and saints, proverbs and parables, literature and life—they all teach us the true meaning of kindness. Sophocles, ancient Greek dramatist, notes: "Kindness gives birth to kindness"; he also holds: "one who knows how to show and to accept kindness will be a better friend than any possession." Jean Jacques Rousseau, the French philosopher, asserts: "What wisdom can you find that is greater than kindness"? Greek writer Aesop affirms: "No act of kindness, no matter how small, is ever wasted." Mark Twain, American author, says: "Kindness is the language which the deaf can hear and the blind can see."

Proverbs from around the world offer insights. "A kind word can warm three months of winter" (Japan). "A kind word is like a spring day" (Russia). "A bit of fragrance always clings to the hand that gives roses" (China). Ancient religious teachers provide additional wisdom. "Kindness in words creates confidence. Kindness in thinking creates profoundness. Kindness in giving creates love" (Lao Tzu). "Teach this triple truth to all: A generous heart, kind speech, and a life of service and compassion are the things which renew humanity" (Buddha).

Contemporary religious leaders also speak insightfully. "Let no one ever come to you without leaving better and happier. Be the living expression of God's kindness: kindness in your face, kindness in your eyes, kindness in your smile" (Mother Teresa). "My religion is very simple. My religion is kindness" (Dalai Lama). "To act lovingly is to begin to feel loving, and certainly to act joyfully brings joy to others which in turn makes one feel joyful. I believe we are called to the duty of delight" (Dorothy Day). "Life's most persistent and urgent question is: What are you doing for others?" (Martin Luther King, Jr.).

Kindness: A Description. Kindness encompasses a range of habits and acts that admits to a wide variety of descriptions. Kindness is a personal quality that enables an individual to be sensitive to the needs of others and to take personal action to meet those needs; it is more than just being nice and agreeable. It is both a quality of one's being and a matter of one's behavior; it encompasses both personal virtue and concomitant action on behalf of others.

Kind people show strength of character; they have generous feelings towards others, not wanting others to suffer; they act from concern for others. A kind person views another's happiness as if it were his own, treating others as he would like to be treated. Like everything else in life, kindness has to be learned. As Eric Hoffer, American social philosopher, wrote: "We are made kind by being kind."

Other descriptions of kindness (Greek: *chrestotes*) include a sense of the ethical, encompassing such traits as honesty, friendliness, generosity, compassion, goodness, justice, and caring. Kindness is described as "an overflow of a thoughtful and selfless love into a realm of speech and action. It is indeed a God-like quality . . . . It is a stable disposition of one's heart that should be carefully cultivated and constantly practiced" (K. McGowan). Try as one might, kindness is more difficult to define succinctly in words than it is to recognize in action!

Kindness: A Virtue. Any exploration of kindness soon leads one to discover that, more than a simple emotion, a spontaneous action, an abstract concept or philosophical idea, kindness is at heart a virtue. Albeit brief, a discussion of "virtue" is necessary to reach to the core of kindness.

Virtue (Latin: *virtus*, "strength of character") is a quality of intellect and character that enables a person to live an honorable and ethically good life. Within the Catholic tradition, the most influential theory of virtue is that of Thomas Aquinas (d. 1274), which in turn is deeply indebted to both Augustine (d. 430) and to Aristotle (d. 322 BC).

They thought that virtue was not simply a single act of bravery or an isolated praiseworthy action; rather, virtue is a habit (Latin, *habitus*, customary mode of behavior). It is a stable quality of intellect, will, and emotions whereby a person can encounter concrete situations in life and respond in an ethically appropriate manner. In brief, both the intellect and will have to be in play. The actual practice of the virtues needs to be grounded in a rational apprehension of what it means to live a morally upright life. Thus, the virtuous individual must be able to apply his knowledge of the good to specific life circumstances through prudential judgment and discernment.

Thomas Aquinas asserted that the practice of virtue was not simply to avoid sins or wrong acts; rather, authentic virtue demands getting into the practice of healthy habits. Such regular activity, in turn, shapes an individual in such a way that he develops dispositions to act in a particular way. Practices form habits. Exercising a virtue helps predispose the person to respond in the same virtuous way in the future. Regular practices become habits, which in turn become deeply ingrained and shape our identity. Our actions determine us as much as we determine our actions. Indeed, kindness begets kindness. We are made kind by being kind.

Kindness Commandments. This presentation now turns from a more theoretical discussion of the virtue of kindness and will focus on ten practical suggestions that, if interiorized, can enhance our progress in practicing the virtue of kindness. Since kindness is a growth process, one does not just get up in the morning and say, "Beginning today, I'm going to be kind." Virtue grows slowly and only through constant exercise. We need to plan our actions so as to become the people we are called by God to be. If we wish to grow in kindness, then we must adopt "kindness exercises"; we seek concrete opportunities to manifest kindness. In addition to these efforts, we realize that even our best intentions will fail if we rely only on our own strength. Growth in virtue needs constant openness to God's assistance.

This very practical approach (following what I call the "ten commandments" to foster kindness) draws its inspiration from the way "kindness" is frequently used in the Bible. Often the word "show" accompanies the word "kindness." A classic example is Jesus' parable of the Good Samaritan (Lk. 10:29–37). The final verses contain the dialogue between the man and Jesus: "Which of these three, do you think, proved himself neighbor to the man who fell into the robbers' hands?" "The one who showed pity on him," the man replied. Jesus said to him, "Go, and do the same yourself." Authentic virtue is always put into concrete actions that "show" compassion to the neighbor.

Friends, as you continue reading, please note that in the subsequent ten sections, you will always find a brief suggestion stated in the form of a command. This will be followed by a short discussion of how this "commandment" can be concretized to promote personal growth in the virtue of kindness.

I. *Meditate on God's kindness.* All world religions promote a variety of virtues, including kindness, by which the adherents of that faith guide their lives. The Judaeo-Christian tradition is rich in its assertions of God's kindness toward his people and the concomitant duty to manifest kindness to one's neighbor. The Psalmist writes: "Give thanks to the Lord, for he is good; his loving kindness endures forever" (Ps. 106:1). Isaiah notes: "With everlasting love I have taken pity on you, says Yahweh, your redeemer" (Is. 54:8). Joel proclaims: "Turn to Yahweh, your God, again, for he is all tenderness and compassion, slow to anger, rich in graciousness" (Joel 2:13).

Jesus himself, sent from the Father, is described as the revelation of "the kindness and love of God our savior for humanity" (Titus 3:4). The Father reveals "the immeasurable riches of his grace in his kindness to us in Christ Jesus" (Eph. 2:7). Jesus is God's kindness in person; his is a ministry of compassion to the little, lonely, least, lost, and last of society, e.g. widow of Naim (Lk. 7:11–17), woman with hemorrhage and Jairus' daughter (Lk. 8:40–56), epileptic demoniac (Lk. 9:37–43), woman caught in adultery (Jn.

8:1–11), etc. Indeed, Jesus invites all the burdened to come to him for rest (Mt. 11:28–30).

Other faith traditions assert the importance of kindness; Christians can also glean insights from them. Confucius urged his followers to "recompense kindness with kindness." Buddhism holds that one of the ten perfections (*paramitas*) is *mettā*, which is usually translated into English as "loving-kindness." The Talmud claims that "deeds of kindness are equal in weight to all the commandments." Muhammad was known for the virtue of Al-Rifq, which in Arabic means: kindness, gentleness, and mildness; his followers are exhorted to imitate his virtues. Religions can mutually promote virtuous living, so the great gift of peace will prosper.

II. *Cultivate an "attitude of gratitude."* All life is gift. We are gifted again and again. All people and events are gifts. Each day is a new gift. Thus, gratitude can never be a single, one-time expression. And, we do not earn life's gifts; God is the source of our richness. Many of these blessings often arrive in and through other persons. This reminds us that gifts are meant for sharing, not for hiding or hoarding. Kindnesses, whatever their form, are concrete ways of expressing our gratitude for the copious—often undeserved—gifts we have received.

Developing our "attitude of gratitude" requires continuous remembering; in this way our past graced moments, big and small, become present and alive in our lives. Like Israel, we must never forget the Lord's deeds (Ps. 78:7; 103:2). This gratitude is not only a fair-weather virtue; prosperous times and difficult moments are equally opportunities to give thanks through deeds of kindness. We are to express and manifest gratitude regularly; then it becomes a habit ingrained in our person. Each act of gratitude makes the next act easier.

Grateful people are at peace with themselves, with others, and with what they have. Gratitude is a sign of a mature and integrated personality. It is reflected in all our activities—especially in our prayer. For Christians, the Eucharist means thanksgiving; its celebration can transform us into loving, grateful, serving persons, permeated with an "attitude of gratitude." We follow Matthew's dictum (Mt. 10:8): "What you have received as a gift, give as a gift."

III. *Appreciate your own goodness.* Kindness to those around you is important, but it only flows out of your own person. Thus, "low self-esteem" can become a hindrance to the practice of kindness. Ask yourself: Are you happy with yourself to the point that you look forward to meeting the day and those persons you will encounter? Or, do you frequently tend to be down on yourself and life? How do we go about finding our true worth, the genuine goodness in ourselves?

We begin with a special effort to examine our own lives and experiences to see what they contain that is of genuine value to help us and others to uplift our existence. We stop putting ourselves and others down. If we take an unbiased look, we will find several basically good things about our person, even in spite of all our problems and confusions. We can begin with the basic goodness of being alive. God has personally created and loved us—individually and by name. God has created us good; and, I like to say, "God does not make junk"! We are precious!

John the Evangelist writes: "Think of the love that the Father has lavished on us, by letting us be called God's children; and that is what we are" (I Jn. 3:1). We are truly loveable, not because of our great personal accomplishments, but because God has loved us. John continues: "Since God has loved us so much, we too should love one another" (I Jn. 4:11). Here is a formula for overcoming some personal blocks to the practice of kindness; pray frequently: "I am your gift, O loving God. In gratitude, let me share my giftedness."

IV. *Empathize with others.* Empathy is the ability to identify with and understand another person's feelings or difficulties. André Gide, French writer, holds that empathy underpins kindness; for him: "True kindness presupposes the faculty of imagining as one's own the suffering and joys of others." Empathy is the ability to walk in the shoes of the other, to see life from his or her perspective. Plato said: "Be kind, for everyone you meet is fighting a hard battle."

Many of us have heard accounts of kind people who empathized with prisoners of war and chose to act with deliberate kindness toward the prisoners. During World War II several Maryknoll priests who were unable to return to their mission in Japan because of the Pacific War went to serve the Japanese interred in POW camps in California; the priests used their ability to speak Japanese to bring comfort, consolation, and guidance to these innocent Japanese who had been interred as a security precaution. The Japanese never forgot the empathetic kindness. Although they remained Buddhists, they regularly sent donations to Maryknoll to support its mission works.

Recently, I experienced the loving concern of a Muslim fisherman named Utol. He regularly supplied fish to the seminary where I was teaching. When he learned that my younger sister was involved in a serious automobile accident and that her life was in danger, he, at great personal inconvenience, searched me out to express his concern. I was deeply moved by the words of faith that he uttered: "I am so sorry to hear the sad news. . . . I want to tell you that I will pray to Allah for your sister's recovery. Allah will help her, I am sure." Indeed, Utol's empathy and kindness brought tears to my eyes. I treasure that experience in my heart!

V. *Practice deliberate kindness.* Our discussions on kindness may sound good in theory, but do "acts of genuine kindness" happen in practice? Unequivocally, the answer is "yes." Myriad acts of "living kindness" are performed each day. We may tend to doubt that altruism is alive when we witness insensitivity and read in the newspapers about how people constantly "use other people." Thus, each of us needs to consciously and purposely decide to practice deliberate kindness, with, of course, the help of the Holy Spirit's grace to prompt us into action. We often underestimate the power of a smile, a touch, a listening ear, a kind word, or even the smallest act of caring to positively impact the life of others.

Acts of deliberate or random kindness often involve the most mundane aspects of daily life. They may be demonstrated by opening the door for an elderly lady, helping a blind person get off the bus, making a personal visit to a friend suffering from Alzheimer's disease, thanking the grocery clerk for her kind service, offering a cold drink to the garbage collector on a hot day. We all could multiply such simple—yet significant—examples drawn from everyday life.

Recently, when I was riding the metro train in Manila, a young man saw me (I'm a senior citizen—though able-bodied) and surrendered his seat. At the next stop he was able to sit again after several people alighted from the train. Then, at the next station a mother and child boarded the train; the young man quickly offered his seat. Before arriving at the next stop which was my destination, I got up and approached the man; I praised and thanked him effusively. I wanted to encourage him and strengthen him to continue his laudatory behavior. In short, practice kindness yourself; praise others who perform kind deeds.

VI. *Employ "kind speech" always.* The tongue and its force for good or evil is graphically described in the New Testament in the Letter of James. "Nobody must imagine that he is religious while . . . not keeping control over his tongue" (1:26). "The tongue is only a tiny part of the body. . . . Think how a small flame can set fire to a huge forest; the tongue is like that. Among all the parts of the body, the tongue is a whole wicked world in itself. . . . We use it to bless the Lord and Father, but we also use it to curse men who are made in God's image: the blessing and the curse come out of the same mouth" (3:5–10).

The tongue can be an instrument of great kindness—as long as it is properly controlled. Kind, sincere words can soothe pain and sorrow, inspire hope in faint hearts, lighten life's burdens, uplift the unfortunate, lessen the bitterness of failure, speak good intentions, express sincere forgiveness, promise love and life-long commitment. Well-chosen speech is one common way of showing kindness, while the opposite use is, unfortunately, also often apparent. Perhaps, this is the reason that James, whose letter lays particular emphasis on the practical good works expected of Christians, wrote so emphatically on the proper use of the tongue.

One could make a long list of practical tips for "kind speech": Think before you speak, considering the effect of your words. Avoid gossipmongers and change the subject when gossip begins. Talk about ideas and events, rather than the faults of others. Use your words and smile to uplift others. Share bad news about people carefully and only if you must. Avoid smart remarks that devastate the ego of others. In conversation, apply the criteria of genuine love found in Paul's "ode to love" in I Corinthians 13. Remember the admonition of Blaise Pascal: "Kind words do not cost much; yet, they accomplish much."

VII. *Judge others compassionately*. Situations inevitably arise when a judgment is necessary. These often require the wisdom of experience and maturity; frequently there are no easy answers. William O'Malley, high school teacher at Fordham Preparatory School in New York, describes such a situation and some possible responses.

"Parents could react in various ways to the shock of hearing their daughter is pregnant: (a) rail and curse, threaten, abuse; (b) offer 'the' answer: 'This is what we're going to do, young lady,' (c) collapse into a swamp of self-recrimination: 'How have I failed?'; or (d) put their arms around her and grieve with her.

157

That is the test of genuine love: 'For the moment, your shame is more important than the shame you've brought on me.' Too many parents routinely resort to 'grounding' . . . instead of sitting down with the kid and saying, 'Okay. Help me understand.'"

Seeking to sympathetically understand a complicated and difficult situation is the "first kindness step" needed in many situations, be they in the family, office, neighborhood or school. Then, in an atmosphere of trust and openness, devoid of rash judgment, the best course of action can be found.

VIII. *Forgive from the heart.* Christian life is lived one kindness at a time—every time we meet another human being. Every day offers dozens of opportunities to be a witness of God's love, even if those ways seem ordinary and unimportant. However, frequently enough, there are situations that call for an element of forgiveness. Whether an offense is minor or serious, the words of Jesus to Peter's question definitely apply: "Lord, how often must I forgive my brother if he wrongs me? As often as seven times?" Then Jesus answers: "Not seven, I tell you, but seventy-seven times" (Mt. 18: 21–22).

Some may think that showing kindness and forgiveness is a sign of weakness or immaturity. However, the exact opposite is true. A person with a reconciling attitude is actually showing deep strength of character. Such one is a person of principle, one who follows core values—often based on his or her faith.

Compassionate forgiveness figures high in Jesus' list of values: "If you forgive others their failings, your heavenly Father will forgive you yours; but if you do not forgive others, your Father will not forgive your failings either" (Mt. 6:14–15). "Be compassionate as your Father is compassionate. Do not judge, and you will not be judged; do not condemn, and you will not be condemned; grant pardon, and you will be pardoned" (Lk. 6:36–37). Share kindness and you will receive kindness.

IX. *Admit your narcissism.* This next "kindness commandment" is actually a "corollary" to number three mentioned above. Practicing the virtue of kindness demands awareness of both one's strengths and weaknesses. Humanly, we are always in danger of succumbing to the downward pull of pride rather than the upward push of grace. Narcissistic tendencies, which focus on my feelings and my needs, are not erased by the waters of baptism. We are very well aware that the leap from self-concern to concern for

159

others is no easy task. Our own needs and pain are real and often feel overwhelming. Yet, Jesus challenges us to loving kindness even when we are not inclined to do so, to care for others in spite of our own afflictions. In the words of Henri Nouwen, we are to be "wounded healers."

Just as all virtues have their opposing side, known as vices, there is an opposite side to kindness. Its three main adversaries are our propensity to be domineering (we wanting control the situation), resentful (we begrudge others credit or recognition), and envious (we are jealous of others' gain, seeing it as our loss). We need to recognize and balance two key facets of our persons: our own negative tendencies (they are real) and the call of Jesus to loving kindness—right in the midst of joy or sorrow, gain or loss. The path of virtue is often a narrow, steep road!

X. *Pray, meditate, seek inner peace.* There is an underlying quality of kindness that is implicit in everything that has been said so far: enormous strength is needed to practice this virtue. This is especially true when dealing with difficult persons or complex situations. Sometimes, we are simply at a loss on how to proceed or what path to take. We might even question if anything we could do would actually better the situation we are in. Where can we find our strength and inner peace?

Personally, I have drawn insight from the concrete approaches of several fellow missioners. Father Bob who serves in Bangladesh says that he humbly goes about each day doing whatever small tasks he can for the sick poor—all in imitation of Jesus whom he receives daily in the Eucharist. Father Frank who works with the garbage pickers and mental patients in southern Philippines follows the same approach. Fathers Bob and Frank, and countless other ordinary people, embody the same faith vision enunciated by Mother Teresa: "Be faithful in small things because it is in them that your strength lies." "Do not think that love, in order to be genuine, has to be extraordinary. What we need is to love without getting tired." "If you can't feed a hundred people, then just feed one." "In this life we cannot do great things. We can only do small things with great love." "Many people mistake our work for our vocation. Our vocation is the love of Jesus." "We are all pencils in the hand of God." Friends, we all need to pray and meditate frequently, using the words of Jesus in the Gospels and the insights of holy persons like Mother Teresa.

Conclusion. One final quotation can bring this essay to a challenging finale. It is drawn from William Penn (1644–1718); he was an English-born American Quaker reformer. "I expect to pass through life but once. If therefore, there be any kindness I can show, or any good thing I can do to any fellow being, let me do it now, and not defer or neglect it, as I shall not pass this way again." I believe Jesus would agree and probably repeat words from his Good Samaritan parable: "Go and do likewise."

26

Bear One Another's Burden

M.J. Riordan

I wonder if no friends were left to me
How I should fare;
How brave the world and all its misery
With none to care.

The doom is not that friendless and alone
We earn our bread;
For that were but to turn our hearts to stone,
Our feet to lead.

It was but meant that friend with friend we go
Adown that road;
That humbly hand to hand we work, and so
To share the load.

Then let me not, dear Lord, forget the plea
Each dawning day,
That altogether lone I may not be
To face the fray.

27

The Two Brothers

Joseph G. Healey

Two brothers wanted to go to a distant country to make their fortune. They asked their father for a blessing, saying, "Father, we are going away to make our fortune. May we have your blessing, please?"

Their father agreed. "Go with my blessing, but on your way put marks on the trees lest you get lost."

After they received the blessing, the two brothers set off on their safari. The older brother entered the forest and, as he made his way through it, cut down some of the trees and made marks on other trees. He did this for the whole length of his journey.

The younger brother took another route. As he was walking along, he came to a house. He knocked on the door, was invited in, and made friends with the children of that family. He stayed there for a while and then continued along on his way, making friends through the whole length of his journey.

Finally, the two brothers returned home. Their father gave them a warm welcome, saying, "How happy I am to see you back home again, my sons, especially since you have returned safely. Wonderful! Now I would like to see the marks that you have left on the trees."

So the father went off with his first-born son. On the way, the son showed his father all the trees that he had cut down and others he had marked along the way. They traveled a long distance without eating and finally returned home empty-handed, as they had set out.

Next, the father set out with his second-born son. During the journey, various friends warmly received the younger son and his father, who were treated as special guests at each place they visited, with goats often slaughtered to prepare a feast to welcome them. When the father and his son returned home, they brought with them many gifts they had received.

Then the father summoned his two sons and said, "Dear sons, I have seen the work that you have done. I will arrange a marriage for the one who has done better."

He turned to the first-born son and said, "My son,

I think you are foolish. You do not know how to take care of people. I told you to put marks on the trees wherever you passed, but you have cut down many trees. Where is the profit in all these felled trees?"

Turning to the second son, he said, "My son, you are clever. I am happy you have left such important marks on your journey. Wherever we passed, we received a fine welcome. This came from your good relationships with the people we visited."

Then he said, "My dear children, now it is time for me to give my reward. I am going to arrange a big feast for my younger son. We will slaughter a cow for him, for my younger son has left good and lasting marks wherever he passed."

28

My Mother's Best Putt

John Shea

"Well, we did it," my teacher announced one day in May when I was in eighth grade—a hundred years ago. "We finished the work for the year. Now we can have fun." We still had three weeks of school left, but Sr. Rosemary had whipped us through the second semester in record time and we had completed all the assigned material.

Fun for Sr. Rosemary was a never-ending series of spelling bees ("Don't forget to repeat the word before you try to spell it"), geography quizzes ("What is the capital of Nigeria?"), and speed math ("Alright, when I say 'go' turn the page and solve the problem. When you are finished, raise your hand.") Sister loved intellectual contests of all types—usually the boys pitted against the girls. Gender wars started early.

I felt all this busy work was really stupid. And I

told people so—especially my mother. Those were the days when kids went home for lunch. As I ate and my mother did things around the kitchen, I complained vociferously and daily. My mother was—as usual—firmly on Sr. Rosemary's side.

"Why do you think it is stupid?" she would ask.

"Because it is," I'd reply. Did I have to explain the obvious?

"Well it's only three weeks. Offer it up," she suggested.

Now "offer it up" was Catholic code for "suffering can't be avoided, so you might as well get something good out of it." Rather than endure meaningless suffering, you could "offer it up"—usually for the "poor souls in purgatory." The idea was that you could gain merits by bearing suffering without complaint and then transfer the benefits to others who needed spiritual help. And nobody needed more help than the poor souls.

However, the redemptive use of my pain did not interest me. I continued my lunchtime assaults on Sr. Rosemary. Several times, my mother warned me that she didn't want to hear any more about it. But I kept it up.

One day, after a morning of supposedly "fun" quizzes, I launched a full-scale attack on the "stupid" way we were wasting time. I was sitting at the table eating a sandwich, and my mother was washing some dishes. She had her back to me, but I noticed her shoulders suddenly arch and move up toward her ears.

I had gotten to her, and I felt a sense of triumph.

But then her shoulders relaxed. Without turning around, she said, "It'll just take a minute."

She went into the bedroom and came out wearing a sweater. "Down in the basement," she ordered.

I wanted to ask what was going on, but for once in my young life I thought I had best keep my mouth shut.

In the basement, my mother pulled out her golf clubs. "Let's go," she said.

Totally confused, I picked up my own clubs and followed behind her. I was having trouble fathoming what was happening. It looked as if I was skipping school to play golf—with my mother no less. She was playing the person feared by every Catholic youth of the time: she was being a "bad companion," luring me away from responsibility.

We lived only six blocks from Columbus Park, a nine-hole Park District course. It cost a quarter for kids and seventy-five cents for adults. As we were walking over to the course, my mother chatted away about this and that. But she did not say one word about school or quizzes or Sr. Rosemary or what we were doing. I kept quiet, waiting for another very large shoe to fall.

On the fourth hole, my mother was about to putt. She had a four-footer. I was holding the flag and waiting. She looked up from the ball and said, "We won't tell anybody about this." Then she smiled.

She made the putt.

Such is the way of kindness.

29

Man Proves, Once Again, That Kindness Can Be a Calling

Steve Hartman

By any logical standard, two years ago Eugene Yoon made the craziest decision of his life.

"I remember kind of just like looking up at the sky and being like, 'God, are you sure about this? 'Cause I'm pretty happy right now,'" Eugene said. "It felt like a calling."

What Eugene felt called to do was one really big random act of kindness. He didn't know who he was supposed to help or how, all he knew was that he had to help someone and it had to be life-altering.

And that's when a video came across his Facebook page.

As we first reported in 2015, it was a video of a guy he never met named Arthur Reñowitzky. After being mugged, shot and paralyzed 10 years ago, Arthur vowed that he would walk again someday. And when Eugene heard about that, he called Arthur immediately.

"He wasn't going to give up until I was walking again," Arthur said.

And Eugene did not have a medical degree. "I have a film degree," he said.

Which makes you wonder then, how was Eugene going to make him walk again? "This is the part . . . I had no idea," he said.

Eventually though, he learned about an exoskeleton device that can help some people walk again. Unfortunately, it costs about $80,000.

So, to pay for it, Eugene quit his job at a research company in Northern California, to hike from the California-Mexico border to Canada.

Along the way he posted videos of the adventure and asked people to donate on social media. Until, 'round about mid-Washington state, Eugene learned that he had reached his fundraising goal.

A few weeks later, Arthur did walk—right into the arms of the total stranger who made it all possible.

"I call him my brother now. We are brothers. I'm just very thankful to have a friend like him," Arthur said. Since his story first aired, Eugene has been looking for another total stranger to help with another huge act of kindness.

And here he is: Alberto Velasquez lives in poverty with 24 family members under one roof.

Eugene met Alberto's family on Skid Row in Los Angeles and then hired Alberto, a skilled seamster, to help start a clothing line called KIN LOV GRA. Proceeds will guarantee Alberto and his family a living wage and fund many other kindness projects to come.

Eugene may have started with a walk, but is now clearly up and running.

Kindly Light

I get much satisfaction from helping others, especially here in Hong Kong. However, I am not comfortable receiving help from others. Still, the kindest thing I can do for others is to let them do something for me. People bring me fruit, cookies, and awful tasting medicine for my ailments. Sometimes they give me a red packet and say, "Buy something to eat." These gifts come from people who are certainly much poorer than I am. But it would be devastating to tell someone, "You are too poor to give me a gift." I need to let people love me and then later figure out how to redistribute the gifts they have given me.

—EUGENE F. THALMAN, MM

30

The Bishop's Candlesticks

Victor Hugo

Once there was a poor young man named Jean Valjean. He lived with his widowed sister and her seven children, supporting them whenever a shopkeeper or farmer needed help. Then one desolating winter, there were simply no jobs. And no food. So one Sunday night, Jean smashed the small window of the baker's shop and stole one loaf of bread.

And he was caught, practically in the act. The hawk-faced judge snarled. "We must make an example of you, young scoundrel. Five years in the galleys! Next!"

So for a pane of glass and a loaf of bread no one would ever eat, Jean was taken to the seaport of Toulon, an iron collar riveted to his neck, and he took his place among the convicts of the great oars of a prison ship. "Stroke, stroke" to the beat of the drum and lash.

And every night the stone prison, the meager food, and the plank bed.

At the end of his fourth year, Jean had a chance to escape and he took it. But after only 36 hours he was caught and hauled back for three more years. In his tenth year he tried again and was caught; three more years. And again, four more years. Finally, after 19 years of torment he was released in the town of Digne and given his severance pay: 119 francs and 15 sous. At whatever inn or shop he stopped at, in his rags and with his yellow convict's passport, he was broomed away. Finally, in desperation he knocked at the door of the parish church.

It was opened by a chubby priest with the open grin of a child. "Oh, my brother!" the priest said. "Come in! I was about to have supper! Madame Magloire, another place please, with the guest silver, for Monsieur . . . ?"

"Number . . . Jean Valjean. I am a convict. But I can pay."

"Nonsense! My name is Bishop Bienvenu, your name is Jean, my brother, come in, come in!" He led Jean into the dining room where the housekeeper was setting a place with a plate, a soup bowl, a wineglass, and the sparkling silverware. So Jean fell to the bread and soup and wine like a wolf while the priest chattered about the cold and lack of food. When they finished, the priest led him to an alcove off his own bedroom where there was a simple bed. As they passed through the kitchen, Madame Magloire was placing the silver in a basket in a cupboard.

"Sleep well, Brother," the priest said and left Jean alone and dumbfounded. For a long time, he could hardly sleep, unused to a full belly, the warm soft bed, restless with the memories, 20 wretched and irretrievable years—the squalor the indignities. the pains, the screaming.

When the church clock tolled three Jean Valjean rose and crept passed the softly snoring priest, into the kitchen. He reached into the cupbord and quietly pulled out the basket of silver and disappeared into the night.

Next morning, while Madame Magloire implored heaven over the lost silver, the bishop sat absently stirring his coffee when suddenly there was a heavy rap on the door, and the bishop rose to answer it. There in the doorway stood two gendarmes with Jean Valjean and an officer with a basket of silver in is hand.

"Ah, my brother, Jean Valjean. . . ."

"You mean . . . ?" the officer said.

"Yes, yes, but I see you took only the silverware. Madame Magloire, would you fetch the silver candlesticks which I also want to give you."

"You gave him . . . ?"

"With all my heart. Go with God, friend Jean." The bishop embraced him and said in a low voice, "Don't forget that you promised to use this money to become an honest man."

Jean Valjean, who didn't remember promising anything, remained speechless. The bishop continued, "Jean Valjean, my brother, you no longer belong to evil, but to good. I buy your soul from you; I withdraw it from black thoughts and the spirit of perdition, and I give it to God." The bishop smiled again, and closed the door.

The officer shrugged at the two bewildered gendarmes and handed the basket to Jean. And left Jean Valjean speechless with a basket of silver in one fist and two silver candlesticks in the other.

31

The Last Leaf

O. Henry

In a little district west of Washington Square the streets have run crazy and broken themselves into small strips called "places." These "places" make strange angles and curves. One Street crosses itself a time or two. An artist once discovered a valuable possibility in this street. Suppose a collector with a bill for paints, paper and canvas should, in traversing this route, suddenly meet himself coming back, without a cent having been paid on account!

So, to quaint old Greenwich Village the art people soon came prowling, hunting for north windows and eighteenth-century gables and Dutch attics and low rents. Then they imported some pewter mugs and a chafing dish or two from Sixth Avenue, and became a "colony."

At the top of a squatty, three-story brick Sue and

Johnsy had their studio. "Johnsy" was familiar for Joanna. One was from Maine; the other from California. They had met at the table d'hôte of an Eighth Street "Delmonico's," and found their tastes in art, chicory salad and bishop sleeves so congenial that the joint studio resulted.

That was in May. In November a cold, unseen stranger, whom the doctors called Pneumonia, stalked about the colony, touching one here and there with his icy fingers. Over on the east side this ravager strode boldly, smiting his victims by scores, but his feet trod slowly through the maze of the narrow and moss-grown "places."

Mr. Pneumonia was not what you would call a chivalric old gentleman. A mite of a little woman with blood thinned by California zephyrs was hardly fair game for the red-fisted, short-breathed old duffer. But Johnsy he smote; and she lay, scarcely moving, on her painted iron bedstead, looking through the small Dutch window-panes at the blank side of the next brick house.

One morning the busy doctor invited Sue into the hallway with a shaggy, grey eyebrow.

"She has one chance in—let us say, ten," he said, as he shook down the mercury in his clinical thermometer. "And that chance is for her to want to live. This way people have of lining-up on the side of the undertaker makes the entire pharmacopoeia look silly. Your little lady has made up her mind that she's not going to get well. Has she anything on her mind?"

"She—she wanted to paint the Bay of Naples someday," said Sue.

"Paint? Bosh! Has she anything on her mind worth thinking twice—a man for instance?"

"A man?" said Sue, with a jew's-harp twang in her voice. "Is a man worth—but, no, doctor; there is nothing of the kind."

"Well, it is the weakness, then," said the doctor. "I will do all that science, so far as it may filter through my efforts, can accomplish. But whenever my patient begins to count the carriages in her funeral procession I subtract 50 percent from the curative power of medicines. If you will get her to ask one question about the new winter styles in cloak sleeves I will promise you a one-in-five chance for her, instead of one in ten."

After the doctor had gone Sue went into the workroom and cried a Japanese napkin to a pulp. Then she swaggered into Johnsy's room with her drawing board, whistling ragtime.

Johnsy lay, scarcely making a ripple under the bedclothes, with her face toward the window. Sue stopped whistling, thinking she was asleep.

She arranged her board and began a pen-and-ink drawing to illustrate a magazine story. Young artists must pave their way to Art by drawing pictures for magazine stories that young authors write to pave their way to Literature.

As Sue was sketching a pair of elegant horseshow riding trousers and a monocle of the figure of the hero, an Idaho cowboy, she heard a low sound, several times repeated. She went quickly to the bedside.

Johnsy's eyes were open wide. She was looking out the window and counting—counting backward.

"Twelve," she said, and little later "eleven"; and then "ten," and "nine"; and then "eight" and "seven," almost together.

Sue look solicitously out of the window. What was there to count? There was only a bare, dreary yard to be seen, and the blank side of the brick house twenty feet away. An old, old ivy vine, gnarled and decayed at the roots, climbed half way up the brick wall. The cold breath of autumn had stricken its leaves from the vine until its skeleton branches clung, almost bare, to the crumbling bricks.

"What is it, dear?" asked Sue.

"Six," said Johnsy, in almost a whisper. "They're falling faster now. Three days ago there were almost a hundred. It made my head ache to count them. But now it's easy. There goes another one. There are only five left now."

"Five what, dear? Tell your Sudie."

"Leaves. On the ivy vine. When the last one falls I must go, too. I've known that for three days. Didn't the doctor tell you?"

"Oh, I never heard of such nonsense," complained Sue, with magnificent scorn. "What have old ivy leaves to do with your getting well? And you used to love that vine so, you naughty girl. Don't be a goosey. Why, the doctor told me this morning that your chances for getting well real soon were—let's see exactly what he said—he said the chances were ten to one! Why, that's almost as good a chance as we have in New York when we ride on the street cars or walk past a new building. Try to take some broth now, and let Sudie go back to her drawing, so she can sell the editor man with it, and buy port wine for her sick child, and pork chops for her greedy self."

"You needn't get any more wine," said Johnsy, keeping her eyes fixed out the window. "There goes another. No, I don't want any broth. That leaves just four. I want to see the last one fall before it gets dark. Then I'll go, too."

"Johnsy, dear," said Sue, bending over her, "will you promise me to keep your eyes closed, and not look out the window until I am done working? I must hand those drawings in by tomorrow. I need the light, or I would draw the shade down."

"Couldn't you draw in the other room?" asked Johnsy, coldly.

"I'd rather be here by you," said Sue. "Besides, I don't want you to keep looking at those silly ivy leaves."

"Tell me as soon as you have finished," said Johnsy, closing her eyes, and lying white and still as a fallen statue, "because I want to see the last one fall. I'm tired of waiting. I'm tired of thinking. I want to turn loose my hold on everything, and go sailing down, down, just like one of those poor, tired leaves."

"Try to sleep," said Sue. "I must call Behrman up to be my model for the old hermit miner. I'll not be gone a minute. Don't try to move 'til I come back."

Old Behrman was a painter who lived on the ground floor beneath them. He was past sixty and had a Michaelangelo's Moses beard curling down from the head of a satyr along with the body of an imp. Behrman was a failure in art. Forty years he had wielded the brush without getting near enough to touch the hem of his Mistress's robe. He had been always about to paint a masterpiece, but had never yet begun it. For several years he had painted nothing except now and then a daub in the line of commerce or advertising. He earned a little by serving as a model to those young artists in the colony who could not pay the price of a professional. He drank gin to excess, and still talked of his coming masterpiece. For the rest he was a fierce little old man, who scoffed terribly at softness in any one, and who regarded himself as especial mastiff-in-waiting to protect the two young artists in the studio above.

Sue found Behrman smelling strongly of juniper berries in his dimly lighted den below. In one corner was a blank canvas on an easel that had been waiting there for twenty-five years to receive the first line of the masterpiece. She told him of Johnsy's fancy, and how she feared she would, indeed, light and fragile as a leaf herself, float away, when her slight hold upon the world grew weaker.

Old Behrman, with his red eyes plainly streaming, shouted his contempt and derision for such idiotic imaginings.

"Vass!" he cried. "Is dere people in de world mit der foolishness to die because leafs dey drop off from a confounded vine? I haf not heard of such a thing. No, I will not bose as a model for your fool hermit-dunderhead. Vy do you allow dot silly pusiness to come in der brain of her? Ach, dot poor leetle Miss Yohnsy."

"She is very ill and weak," said Sue, "and the fever has left her mind morbid and full of strange fancies. Very well, Mr. Behrman, if you do not care to pose for me, you needn't. But I think you are a horrid old—old flibbertigibbet."

"You are just like a woman!" yelled Behrman. "Who said I will not bose? Go on. I come mit you. For half an hour I haf peen trying to say dot I am ready to bose. Gott! dis is not any blace in which one so goot as Miss Yohnsy shall lie sick. Some day I vill baint a masterpiece, and ve shall all go away. Gott! yes."

Johnsy was sleeping when they went upstairs. Sue pulled the shade down to the window-sill, and motioned Behrman into the other room. In there they peered out the window fearfully at the ivy vine. Then they looked at each other for a moment without speaking. A persistent, cold rain was falling, mingled with snow. Behrman, in his old blue shirt, took his seat as the hermit miner on an upturned kettle for a rock.

When Sue awoke from an hour's sleep the next morning she found Johnsy with dull, wide-open eyes staring at the drawn green shade.

"Pull it up; I want to see," she ordered, in a whisper.

Wearily Sue obeyed.

But, lo! after the beating rain and fierce gusts of wind that had endured through the livelong night, there yet stood out against the brick wall one ivy leaf. It was the last one on the vine. Still dark green near its stem, with its serrated edges tinted with the yellow of dissolution and decay, it hung bravely from the branch some twenty feet above the ground.

"It is the last one," said Johnsy. "I thought it would surely fall during the night. I heard the wind. It will fall today, and I shall die at the same time."

"Dear, dear!" said Sue, leaning her worn face down to the pillow, "think of me, if you won't think of yourself. What would I do?"

But Johnsy did not answer. The lonesomest thing in all the world is a soul when it is making ready to go on its mysterious, far journey. The fancy seemed to possess her more strongly as one by one the ties that bound her to friendship and to earth were loosed.

The day wore away, and even through the twilight they could see the lone ivy leaf clinging to its stem against the wall. And then, with the coming of the night the north wind was again loosed, while the rain still beat against the windows and pattered down from the low Dutch eaves.

When it was light enough Johnsy, the merciless, commanded that the shade be raised.

The ivy leaf was still there.

Johnsy lay for a long time looking at it. And then she called to Sue, who was stirring her chicken broth over the gas stove.

"I've been a bad girl, Sudie," said Johnsy. "Something has made that last leaf stay there to show me how wicked I was. It is a sin to want to die. You may bring me a little broth now, and some milk with a little port in it, and—no; bring me a hand-mirror first, and then pack some pillows about me, and I will sit up and watch you cook."

And hour later she said:

"Sudie, some day I hope to paint the Bay of Naples."

The doctor came in the afternoon, and Sue had an

excuse to go into the hallway as he left.

"Even chances," said the doctor, taking Sue's thin, shaking hand in his. "With good nursing you'll win." And now I must see another case I have downstairs. Behrman, his name is—some kind of an artist, I believe. Pneumonia, too. He is an old, weak man, and the attack is acute. There is no hope for him; but he goes to the hospital today to be made more comfortable."

The next day the doctor said to Sue: "She's out of danger. You won. Nutrition and care now—that's all."

And that afternoon Sue came to the bed where Johnsy lay, contentedly knitting a very blue and very useless woolen shoulder scarf, and put one arm around her, pillows and all.

"I have something to tell you, white mouse," she said. "Mr. Behrman died of pneumonia today in the hospital. He was ill only two days. The janitor found him the morning of the first day in his room downstairs helpless with pain. His shoes and clothing were wet through and icy cold. They couldn't imagine where he had been on such a dreadful night. And then they found a lantern, still lighted, and a ladder that had been dragged from its place, and some scattered brushes, and a palette with green and yellow colors mixed on it, and—look out the window, dear, at the last ivy leaf on the wall. Didn't you wonder why it never fluttered or moved when the wind blew? Ah, darling, it's Behrman's masterpiece—he painted it there the night that the last leaf fell."

32

An Angel in Disguise

T.S. Arthur

Idleness, vice, and intemperance had done their miserable work, and the dead mother lay cold and still amid her wretched children. She had fallen upon the threshold of her own door in a drunken fit, and died in the presence of her frightened little ones.

Death touches the spring of our common humanity. This woman had been despised, scoffed at, and angrily denounced by nearly every man, woman, and child in the village; but now, as the fact of her death was passed from lip to lip, in subdued tones, pity took the place of anger, and sorrow of denunciation. Neighbors went hastily to the old tumble-down hut, in which she had secured little more than a place of shelter from summer heats and winter cold: some with grave-clothes for a decent interment of the body; and some with food for the half-starving children, three in number. Of these, John, the oldest, a boy of twelve, was a stout lad, able to earn his living with any farmer. Kate, between ten and eleven, was a bright, active girl, out of whom something clever might be made, if in good hands; but poor little Maggie, the youngest, was hopelessly diseased. Two years before a fall from a window had injured her spine, and she had not been able to leave her bed since, except when lifted in the arms of her mother.

"What is to be done with the children?" That was the chief question now. The dead mother would go underground, and be forever beyond all care or concern of the villagers. But the children must not be left to starve. After considering the matter, and talking it over with his wife, farmer Jones said that he would take John, and do well by him, now that his mother was out of the way; and Mrs. Ellis, who had been looking out for a bound girl, concluded that it would be charitable in her to make choice of Katy, even though she was too young to be of much use for several years.

"I could do much better, I know," said Mrs. Ellis; "but as no one seems inclined to take her, I must act from a sense of duty. I expect to have trouble with the child; for she's an undisciplined thing—used to having her own way."

But no one said "I'll take Maggie." Pitying glances were cast on her wan and wasted form and thoughts were troubled on her account. Mothers brought cast-off garments and, removing her soiled and ragged clothes, dressed her in clean attire. The sad eyes and patient face of the little one touched many hearts, and even knocked at them for entrance. But none opened to take her in. Who wanted a bed-ridden child?

"Take her to the poorhouse," said a rough man, of whom the question "What's to be done with Maggie?" was asked. "Nobody's going to be bothered with her."

"The poorhouse is a sad place for a sick and helpless child," answered one.

"For your child or mine," said the other, lightly speaking; "but for this brat it will prove a blessed change, she will be kept clean, have healthy food, and be doctored, which is more than can be said of her past condition."

There was reason in that, but still it didn't satisfy. The day following the day of death was made the day of burial. A few neighbors were at the miserable hovel, but none followed the dead cart as it bore the unhonored remains to its pauper grave. Farmer Jones, after the coffin was taken out, placed John in his wagon and drove away, satisfied that he had done his part. Mrs. Ellis spoke to Kate with a hurried air, "Bid your sister goodbye," and drew the tearful children apart ere scarcely their lips had touched in a sobbing farewell. Hastily others went out, some glancing at Maggie, and some resolutely refraining from a look, until all had gone. She was alone! Just beyond the threshold Joe Thompson, the wheelwright, paused, and said to the blacksmith's wife, who was hastening off with the rest,—

"It's a cruel thing to leave her so."

"Then take her to the poorhouse: she'll have to go there," answered the blacksmith's wife, springing away, and leaving Joe behind.

For a little while the man stood with a puzzled air; then he turned back, and went into the hovel again. Maggie with painful effort, had raised herself to an upright position and was sitting on the bed, straining her eyes upon the door out of which all had just departed. A vague terror had come into her thin white face.

"O, Mr. Thompson!" she cried out, catching her suspended breath, "don't leave me here all alone!"

Though rough in exterior, Joe Thompson, the

wheelwright, had a heart, and it was very tender in some places. He liked children, and was pleased to have them come to his shop, where sleds and wagons were made or mended for the village lads without a draft on their hoarded sixpences.

"No, dear," he answered, in a kind voice, going to the bed, and stooping down over the child, "You sha'n't be left here alone." Then he wrapped her with the gentleness almost of a woman, in the clean bedclothes which some neighbor had brought; and, lifting her in his strong arms, bore her out into the air and across the field that lay between the hovel and his home.

Now, Joe Thompson's wife, who happened to be childless, was not a woman of saintly temper, nor much given to self-denial for others' good, and Joe had well-grounded doubts touching the manner of greeting he should receive on his arrival. Mrs. Thompson saw him approaching from the window, and with ruffling feathers met him a few paces from the door, as he opened the garden gate, and came in. He bore a precious burden, and he felt it to be so. As his arms held the sick child to his breast, a sphere of tenderness went out from her, and penetrated his feelings. A bond had already corded itself around them both, and love was springing into life.

"What have you there?" sharply questioned Mrs. Thompson.

Joe felt the child start and shrink against him. He did not reply, except by a look that was pleading and cautionary, that said, "Wait a moment for explanations, and be gentle"; and, passing in, carried Maggie to the small chamber on the first floor, and laid her on a bed. Then, stepping back, he shut the door, and stood face to face with his vinegar-tempered wife in the passage-way outside.

"You haven't brought home that sick brat!" Anger and astonishment were in the tones of Mrs. Joe Thompson; her face was in a flame.

"I think women's hearts are sometimes very hard," said Joe. Usually Joe Thompson got out of his wife's way, or kept rigidly silent and non-combative when she fired up on any subject; it was with some surprise, therefore, that she now encountered a firmly-set countenance and a resolute pair of eyes.

"Women's hearts are not half so hard as men's!"

Joe saw, by a quick intuition, that his resolute bearing had impressed his wife and he answered quickly, and with real indignation, "Be that as it may, every woman at the funeral turned her eyes steadily from the sick child's face, and when the cart went off with her dead mother, hurried away, and left her alone in that old hut, with the sun not an hour in the sky."

"Where were John and Kate?" asked Mrs. Thompson.

"Farmer Jones tossed John into his wagon, and drove off. Katie went home with Mrs. Ellis; but nobody wanted the poor sick one. 'Send her to the poorhouse,' was the cry."

"Why didn't you let her go, then. What did you bring her here for?"

"She can't walk to the poorhouse," said Joe; "somebody's arms must carry her, and mine are strong enough for that task."

"Then why didn't you keep on? Why did you stop here?" demanded the wife.

"Because I'm not apt to go on fools' errands. The Guardians must first be seen, and a permit obtained."

There was no gainsaying this.

"When will you see the Guardians?" was asked, with irrepressible impatience.

"To-morrow."

"Why put it off till to-morrow? Go at once for

the permit, and get the whole thing off of your hands to-night."

"Jane," said the wheelwright, with an impressiveness of tone that greatly subdued his wife, "I read in the Bible sometimes, and find much said about little children. How the Savior rebuked the disciples who would not receive them; how he took them up in his arms, and blessed them; and how he said that 'whosoever gave them even a cup of cold water should not go unrewarded.' Now, it is a small thing for us to keep this poor motherless little one for a single night; to be kind to her for a single night; to make her life comfortable for a single night."

The voice of the strong, rough man shook, and he turned his head away, so that the moisture in his eyes might not be seen. Mrs. Thompson did not answer, but a soft feeling crept into her heart.

"Look at her kindly, Jane; speak to her kindly," said Joe. "Think of her dead mother, and the loneliness, the pain, the sorrow that must be on all her coming life." The softness of his heart gave unwonted eloquence to his lips.

Mrs. Thompson did not reply, but presently turned towards the little chamber where her husband had deposited Maggie; and, pushing open the door, went quietly in. Joe did not follow; he saw that her state had changed, and felt that it would be best to leave her alone with the child. So he went to his shop, which stood near the house, and worked until dusky evening released him from labor. A light shining through the little chamber windows was the first object that attracted Joe's attention on turning towards the house: it was a good omen. The path led him by the windows and, when opposite, he could not help pausing to look in. It was now dark enough outside to screen him from observation. Maggie lay, a little raised on the pillow with the lamp shining full upon her face. Mrs. Thompson was sitting by the bed, talking to the child; but her back was towards the window, so that her countenance was not seen. From Maggie's face, therefore, Joe must read the character of their intercourse. He saw that her eyes were intently fixed upon his wife; that now and then a few words came, as if in answers from her lips; that her expression was sad and tender; but he saw nothing of bitterness or pain. A deep-drawn breath was followed by one of relief, as a weight lifted itself from his heart.

On entering, Joe did not go immediately to the little chamber. His heavy tread about the kitchen brought his wife somewhat hurriedly from the room where she had been with Maggie. Joe thought it best not to refer to the child, nor to manifest any concern in regard to her.

"How soon will supper be ready?" he asked.

"Right soon," answered Mrs. Thompson, beginning to bustle about. There was no asperity in her voice.

After washing from his hands and face the dust and soil of work, Joe left the kitchen, and went to the little bedroom. A pair of large bright eyes looked up at him from the snowy bed; looked at him tenderly, gratefully, pleadingly. How his heart swelled in his bosom! With what a quicker motion came the heart-beats! Joe sat down, and now, for the first time, examining the thin frame carefully under the lamp light, saw that it was an attractive face, and full of a childish sweetness which suffering had not been able to obliterate.

"Your name is Maggie?" he said, as he sat down and took her soft little hand in his.

"Yes, sir." Her voice struck a chord that quivered in a low strain of music.

"Have you been sick long?"

"Yes, sir." What a sweet patience was in her tone!

"Has the doctor been to see you?"

"He used to come."

"But not lately?"

"No, sir."

"Have you any pain?"

"Sometimes, but not now."

"When had you pain?"

"This morning my side ached, and my back hurt when you carried me."

"It hurts you to be lifted or moved about?"

"Yes, sir."

"Your side doesn't ache now?"

"No, sir."

"Does it ache a great deal?"

"Yes, sir; but it hasn't ached any since I've been on this soft bed."

"The soft bed feels good."

"O, yes, sir—so good!" What a satisfaction, mingled with gratitude, was in her voice!

"Supper is ready," said Mrs. Thompson, looking into the room a little while afterwards.

Joe glanced from his wife's face to that of Maggie; she understood him, and answered,—

"She can wait until we are done; then I will bring her somethings to eat." There was an effort at indifference on the part of Mrs. Thompson, but her husband had seen her through the window, and understood that the coldness was assumed. Joe waited, after sitting down to the table, for his wife to introduce the subject uppermost in both of their thoughts; but she kept silent on that theme, for many minutes, and he maintained a like reserve. At last she said, abruptly,—

"What are you going to do with that child?"

"I thought you understood me that she was to go to the poorhouse," replied Joe, as if surprised at her question.

Mrs. Thompson looked rather strangely at her husband for some moments, and then dropped her eyes. The subject was not again referred to during the meal. At its close, Mrs. Thompson toasted a slice of bread, and softened it with milk and butter; adding to this a cup of tea, she took them into Maggie, and held the small waiter, on which she had placed them, while the hungry child ate with every sign of pleasure.

"Is it good?" asked Mrs. Thompson, seeing with what a keen relish the food was taken.

The child paused with the cup in her hand, and answered with a look of gratitude that awoke to new life old human feelings which had been slumbering in her heart for half a score of years.

"We'll keep her a day or two longer; she is so weak and helpless," said Mrs. Joe Thompson, in answer to her husband's remark, at breakfast-time on the next morning, that he must step down and see the Guardians of the Poor about Maggie.

"She'll be so much in your way," said Joe.

"I sha'n't mind that for a day or two. Poor thing!"

Joe did not see the Guardians of the Poor on that day, on the next, nor on the day following. In fact, he never saw them at all on Maggie's account, for in less than a week Mrs. Joe Thompson would as soon leave thought of taking up her own abode in the almshouse as sending Maggie there.

What light and blessing did that sick and helpless child bring to the home of Joe Thompson, the poor wheelwright! It had been dark, and cold, and miserable there for a long time just because his wife had nothing to love and care for out of herself, and so became sore, irritable, ill-tempered, and self-afflicting in the desolation of her woman's nature. Now the sweetness of that sick child, looking ever to her in love, patience, and gratitude, was as honey to her soul, and she carried her in her heart as well as in her arms, a precious burden. As for Joe Thompson, there was not a man in all the neighborhood who drank daily of a more precious wine of life than he. An angel had come into his house, disguised as a sick, helpless, and miserable child, and filled all its dreary chambers with the sunshine of love.

Kindly Light

*On a steep and rocky path in Africa, I encoun-
tered a small girl who carried on her back her little
brother. "My child," I said to her, "you carry a heavy
burden." She looked at me and said: "I carry not a
heavy burden. I carry my brother!" I was speechless.
The words of this child sank deep into my heart.
When people's troubles seem to weigh me down to
a point where I nearly lose heart, the words of the
child come back to me: "I carry not a heavy burden.
I carry my brother!"*

—AFRICAN PARABLE

33

The Kindness of Strangers

Barbara E. Reid

There are all kinds of good reasons for not stopping to help a stranger: I have other pressing obligations. It's dangerous—what if the robbers are still lurking and attack me? I don't have any professional skills or resources to help this person. If I move him and make his injuries worse he might sue me. And on and on.

I can easily talk myself out of any good deed, just like the scholar of the law in today's Gospel. He knew what to do. He knew what his religious convictions prompted him to do. He could recite the law perfectly. He also knew what his heart was urging him to do. He just needed somebody to reassure him that his rationalizations were well founded and that no one would expect him to do anything for some stranger in need.

It would have been easy for Jesus to give him the

answer he wanted: "Yes, of course you're right. He is not your responsibility. Someone better equipped will tend to him." But he does not. Jesus knows it will not be easy for the scholar to hear his answer. Better than rational arguments, a story will help the scholar move out of his head and listen to his heart. There is, however, a twist to the story that Jesus tells. It is not a straightforward tale about someone like the scholar who is "moved with compassion" that he might easily emulate.

The complication is that the scholar of the law would never identify with a hated Samaritan. More likely he would see himself in the person in need at the side of the road. From that perspective, he would watch in horror as the priest and Levite, the ones he would expect to act with pastoral attention, pass him by while justifying themselves. To receive lavish aid after that from a despised Samaritan breaks open the strictures of his heart, as he experiences a flood of grace from this unexpected source.

The parable asks the scholar, stripped of his defenses, to accept the ways in which divine compassion and grace have been showered upon him in undeserved ways. From this place, he could then be prompted to extend these to others.

The question is not really, "Who is my neighbor?" Deep down the scholar knows that each human being and every creature are neighbor and kin, all relying on one another in the fragile web of life. The scholar does not want to admit this to himself because of what it will ask of him. In the depths of his heart, however, he knows what he must do to aid a fellow traveler in need. It is not really too hard or too mysterious to figure out, as Moses tells the Israelites in the first reading. You do not need someone to "go up in the sky" or "cross the sea." How to live out God's way as elaborated in the Scriptures is actually "something very near to you, already in your mouths and in your hearts; you have only to carry it out," as Moses asserts.

Sometimes we need to be helped out of our rationalizations for not doing what our listening heart prompts us to do. At other times we are asked to be the one who can speak truth lovingly to a friend who struggles to do what compassion asks of them.

Heeding the voice of God to know what is the right action and the right time requires deep listening, in contemplative silent prayer, in honest conversation with trusted friends and in openness to hearing the cacophonous cries of needy neighbors at hand and throughout the globe. We do not know whether the scholar of the law let go of trying to justify himself and was able to "go and do likewise." The parable remains open-ended, inviting us to hear it addressed to ourselves. How will it end?

34

We Are Trying to Make People Happy

Dorothy Day

A few years ago I had to call in a woman doctor, an exile, who had been in a concentration camp in Germany for refusing to sterilize epileptic children. She was taking care of one of the women in the house. As she left she said, recognizing the apparent hopelessness of our work for the most destitute, "The only thing you can do for these sick and aged ones is to make them happy." I have often thought of that since, when people have asked us about the work, what we were trying to do; it seemed very simple to say, "We are trying to make people happy." Father Faber has three conferences in one of his published volumes on kindness. Kindness seems a simple enough virtue, little of the heroic about it, and rather naïve and fatuous, not very much to the point these days when righteous wrath and grim fortitude seem to be more in order. But these conferences make good spiritual reading.

We want to be happy, we want others to be happy, we want to see some of this joy of life which children have, we want to see people intoxicated with God, or just filled with the good steady joy of knowing that Christ is King and that we are His flock and He has prepared for us a kingdom, and that God loves us as a father loves his children, as a bridegroom loves his bride, and that eye hath not seen nor ear heard what God hath prepared for us!

35

Try a Little Kindness

Peter Schineller

In one horrendous plane crash in December 2005, Loyola Jesuit College in Abuja, Nigeria, lost sixty students. I was president of the college. As soon as I could, I traveled to Port Harcourt to be with and to pray with the parents, siblings, relatives and friends of those who were killed. It was no easy mission. Yet because of the deep Christian faith and love of these parents, the meeting took a surprising turn. Parents who had lost one, two or, in one case, three children reached out to me with compassion and kindness. Even as I tried to console them for the loss of their precious children, many tried to console me, saying that as president of the college, I had lost 60 children! Such kindness and compassion, such an ability to reach out beyond their own grief, I will never forget.

This Lent and every Lent, we Christians pro-
fess that "the kindness and generous love of God
our Savior has appeared" (Ti 3:4). Words like love,
power, light, truth and justice are often employed to
describe the coming of God, but the Letter to Titus
uses the word kindness. Perhaps we should take this
as a special challenge this season: to show more of the
kindness of God. It is something the parents in Port
Harcourt did even in the depths of grief. As St. John
Chrysostom writes: "We must be more kind than just.
Kindness alone reconciles."

In traditional Catholic teaching, kindness is the
virtue opposite the vice of envy. An envious person
is unappreciative, resentful, tries to tear down others
and takes secret satisfaction at the misfortune of others. When tempted toward envy, what is the alternative? "Try a Little Kindness," sang Glen Campbell.
Kindness entails an ability to reach out beyond our
own situation, good or bad, to show goodness and
compassion to others.

Abraham Lincoln once echoed the writings of St.
Francis de Sales when he said: as "a drop of honey
catches more flies than a gallon of gall, so with men. If
you would win a man to your cause, first convince him
that you are his sincere friend." Many may recall a line

by former president George H. W. Bush, who in his 1988 Republican National Convention acceptance speech called for "a kinder and gentler nation." Today, under the leadership of a new president, we still hope to move toward this kinder, gentler nation. Yet such change begins with the individual. Where and how can we be kinder and gentler—with our family and children, with our neighbors and strangers, with fellow drivers on the highways or walking the streets of our cities?

Many times in Africa I was called up short for not properly and kindly greeting people. In my brusque U.S. manner, I would rush to the heart of the matter in making a request: "One ticket, two eggs, or how much is this?" The response was a kinder, gentler greeting: "Good morning, Father." Only then could we do business. Greetings are important. Might we not offer such informal greetings as a pleasant surprise at the checkout counter, to the bus driver or bank teller or the police officer at the mall? Might we not listen to our children or a neighbor more patiently and set aside our automatic answers and solutions? When we do speak, might we heed the advice of Adolfo Nicolás, superior general of the Jesuits, who said that before speaking, you should ask three questions about what you will say: "Is it true, is it kind and gentle, and is it good for others?"

Rabbi Abraham Joshua Heschel saw the beauty of kindness: "When I was young, I admired clever people. Now that I am old, I admire kind people." And St. Paul urged the Christians of Rome to "remain in his [God's] kindness" (Rom 11:22).

Lent is the Christian's journey with Jesus to Jerusalem. The Gospel of Matthew says of Jesus that "a bruised reed he will not break, a smoldering wick he will not quench until he brings justice to victory" (12:20); Jesus is "meek and humble of heart" (11:29). This Lent let us try to put on the mind and heart of Jesus Christ. It is an appropriate time to show forth God's kindness, and at the very least to "try a little kindness."

36

My Heart Ran Forth

Jessica Powers

My heart ran forth on little feet of music
to keep the new commandment.
(O feast and frolic of awakening spring!)
It would beguile the world to be a garden
with seeds of one refrain: *My little children,
love one another*, so my heart would sing.

But wisdom halted it, out far afield,
asked: did you sow this seed
around your house, or in the neighbor's garden
or any nearby acreage of need?
No? Then it will not grow in outer places.
Love has its proper soil, its native land;
its first roots fasten on the near-at-hand.

Back toward the house from which I deftly fled,
down neighbors' lanes, across my father's barley
my heart brought home its charity. It said:
love is a simple plant like a Creeping Charlie;
once it takes root its talent is to spread.

Kindly Lights

He who sows courtesy reaps friendship, and he who plants kindness gathers love.

—Saint Basil

When I was a boy and I would see scary things in the news, my mother would say to me, "Look for the helpers. You will always find people who are helping." To this day, especially in times of "disaster," I remember my mother's words and I am always comforted by realizing that there are still so many helpers—so many crying people in this world.

—Fred Rogers

Be kind, for everyone you meet is fighting a great battle.

—Philo of Alexandria

37

Bishop Morrie Says It's Not About the Soup

Michael Leach

Many people are talking about the poor, but very few people talk to the poor."
—MOTHER TERESA

I eat a sloppy joe in the community kitchen with my classmate Morrie, bishop of Paris, Kansas, then follow him around as he talks with his thirty-six guests.

Morrie sneaks up behind a little girl sitting at a big round table with her mother and squeezes her shoulders. The girl startles and holds back a smile. "I know who you are, Father!"

"How do you solve a problem like Maria?" Morrie sings badly. "She climbs a tree and scrapes her knee and waltzes on her way to Mass and dooby dooby doo, what are we gonna do?"

"Maybe we give her to you, Padre," says her mother. "She can work for the church and the sisters look after her."

"Noo-oo," Maria says.

"I don't blame you," Morrie says.

"Are you helping out today, Norma?" he asks her mom.

"Sí. I help Jane stock the bookshelves today. Then I go help my lady."

"Norma is a caregiver," Morrie tells me. "She works two jobs, taking care of old people. She volunteers here when she can."

"Father," the girl says, "I bought something today."

"Brought," her mother says. "You brought something today."

"Wonderful. What is it?"

"You won't laugh?

"Only if you do."

Maria holds up a soft blue blanket. "My blankie," she says. "I don't need it anymore. Someone else can have it."

"She slept with it four years," Norma says. "Never let it go. It makes her feel safe."

"Now it can make someone else safe," Maria says.

"Maria, this is a wonderful gift. May I give you a

hug? OK with you, Norma?" Both Maria and Norma get up.

"Do you know that people need three hugs a day just to survive, six to be healthy, and twelve to grow strong? Did I introduce you two to my friend Mike?"

"I know," Norma says as if she's done this gig many times before. "Group hug!"

The four of us group hug, our foreheads touching. "Hold it ten seconds," Morrie says. "All your stress will disappear."

Ten seconds later, I feel like I had a ten-minute massage.

We bid adieu to Norma and Maria. In the next hour, Morrie spends time with all the guests in the room. He smiles at every one of them. He hugs more than a few and whispers to one of them to call Marge for an appointment to talk about it some more.

My back hurts and I sit down while Morrie continues to work the room. The homeless, those down on their luck, and families just getting by eat together with diocesan staff at tables with white tablecloths and ceramic dishes. The room is as big as a basketball court. Soon after he became bishop of Paris in 1998, Morrie converted this once abandoned meatpacking plant into a Diocesan Center. Most of the building still smells of sheep, but the kitchen is fresher than an empty bottle of Lysol. The two floors above have living quarters and offices for two priests, three sisters, and seven laypeople who help Morrie run the second smallest diocese in the United States. He likes to brag that before he got here Paris was the first smallest.

A plaque on the stone wall next to the doorway of the center reads:

"The bread in your box belongs to the hungry. The cloak in your closet belongs to the naked. The shoes you do not wear belong to the barefoot. The money in your vault belongs to the destitute."—*St. Basil the Great*

The first-floor kitchen is open five days a week, from 10:30 a.m. to 12:30 p.m. Volunteers cook and serve the meals. The guests are also welcome to take home canned goods or baked bread from the bookshelves along one wall, plus cartons of milk in three packinghouse fridges, and clothes, shoes or toys neatly arranged on folding tables at the far end. The guests, aware of their blessings—and no doubt the words of St. Basil, which is also the name of the tiny basilica on the edge of the prairie—bring goods and gifts themselves whenever they can. That, I guess, is why Maria brought her blankie for someone else to feel safe.

The last guests leave, and Morrie pulls up a chair next to mine. "Want a Coke?" he asks.

"No, but you look like you could use one."

"I'm good."

"You know," I tell him. "This is really awesome. Do a lot of dioceses have soup kitchens like this?"

"I like to call it a community kitchen. It's not about the soup."

"I did some research before I flew out here. I read that 50 million Americans, mostly the working poor, have a hard time putting food on the table. Do you think the church could do more?"

"I don't think about that."

We sit in silence for a while. Then Morrie says, "Let's go up to my room for a Coke."

As we lumber by the tables with clothes and shoes and toys, I ask him, "How do you know people won't take stuff they don't need?"

"Honor."

"Does it happen though?"

"It doesn't matter. It's not about the stuff."

"What is it about then?"

Morrie smiles at me.

38

What Have You Done for Someone Today?

Kelli M. Wheeler

Momservation: *"Kindness doesn't cost a damn thing. Sprinkle that s—t everywhere."*
—Unknown

Is anybody else a little worried about humanity right now?

The senseless acts of hatred?

The violent deaths of so many innocents?

The depravity in the name of God?

Anyone else having a hard time feeling optimistic? Anyone else feeling helpless and impotent in the face of such a global and collective forgetting that all lives matter?

My gut instinct is to turn off the news, quit reading the paper, get off the grid, and hide under the covers from the constant stream of negativity.

But like children hiding under the covers from the Closet Monster, we all know that doesn't make it go away. Getting up, opening that closet, and bravely confronting your fears is what makes our anxieties go away.

I don't want to cower in the darkness. I want to stand arms wide, face tilted to the sun soaking up the light.

I refuse to believe hate wins. I have faith that love is always greater than hate.

So what is the first step forward toward the light?

Doing something kind for someone else. Like a pebble thrown into the water rippling throughout the entire pond, it doesn't take much to make a difference:

- Call your grandma
- Tell a stranger they look nice
- Roll your neighbor's garbage cans in
- Invite your in-laws over for dinner
- Help an elderly shopper at the grocery store
- Pay for the coffee of the person behind you in the drive-thru
- Tell your spouse why you appreciate them
- Give an old friend an actual date to the Let's-Get-Together-Sometime

- Play with the dog as long as it wants to
- Tell a child how talented or smart they are

The possibilities for simple acts of kindness are endless! And what if each and every day, as part of our worldly routine, as vital as eating, drinking and sleeping, we asked ourselves: *What have I done for someone today?*

And then we went about and made sure we could answer that with as many acts of kindness as possible.

Now there's something that should be making the news. Let's try it.

39

Blessings of Kindness

Peter C. Phan

I was invited to deliver a lecture at a conference on "World Christianity" and its encounter with other religions at the University of Payap, a Church of Christ in Thailand institution, located in Chiang Mai, a city of enchanting beauty in mountainous northwest Thailand. As customary during academic conferences, there was a free day for sightseeing. Participants were given a tour of Wat Phrathat Doi Suthep, one of the most famous Buddhist pagodas in Thailand, built by King Keu Naone of the Lanna Kingdom in 1383 on a mountain at 1,676 meters above the city of Chiang Mai. Dominating the whole pagoda, which is reached by mounting 309 steps, is a monumental golden statue of a sitting Buddha in serene meditation.

Throngs of pilgrims, young and old, women and

men, rich and poor, ritually circumambulated the statue in prayerful silence, hands clasped at their chests. Others stood in front of the Buddha, incense sticks in their hands, eyes closed, lips murmuring prayers. There was of course the usual number of tourists, but the vast majority were pious faithful worshiping in utter devotion. There was none of the hustling and chattering I have seen at Catholic pilgrimage centers and even in Saint Peter's Basilica in Rome. The atmosphere was suffused with an awe-inspiring aura of sacredness. I was told that on certain feasts, pilgrims would go on foot, sometimes on their knees, from the bottom of the mountain up to the monastery, a pilgrimage that would take days.

After the conference, I stayed another day to see the city of Chiang Mai. I hiked to one of the most famous pagodas mentioned in the tour guide, Wat U-Mong, just on the outskirts of the city. There were heavy, smoke-spewing traffic and ear-splitting din around the pagoda, but inside the pagoda enclosure, there was an eerie peace and tranquility. There were several small pagodas where people came in and out for prayer and a garden with Buddhist proverbs in Thai and English on display on the trees to help the faithful meditate as they walk along the path. Deep silence reigned everywhere on this sacred ground; even birds seemed to cease twittering.

In the middle of the compound stood the main pagoda, majestic and magnificent. In it there were several statues of the Buddha and his disciples, with a huge golden Buddha placed at the center of a high stage near the back. On the left side there was an altar on which there was a sitting statue of Kwan Yin, commonly known as the Goddess of Mercy, whom many Asian Catholics regard as the equivalent of Mother Mary. As I walked toward it, I saw a young woman sitting in a lotus position a short distance in front of the statue, her head slightly bowed. Not to disturb her, I moved quietly to the back and sat on the floor about twenty feet behind her. Intrigued by this figure immersed in prayer, I decided to stay for a while. For nearly three-quarters of an hour, the young woman sat, wrapped in prayer and meditation, not a limb twitching, not a turning of the head, preternaturally still, like the unrippled water of an autumnal pond, under the loving gaze of the Buddha of Compassion, as people walked by. I was irresistibly moved to pray—to the Christian God and to Kwan Yin—by this Buddhist devotee. When I left, the young woman was still praying there, for how much longer I would never know.

I call all these opportunities, and countless others, "blessings" because I consider them to be God's gracious gifts, as precious as the gift of the Christian faith. I do not, however, claim to have any epistemological privilege or superior knowledge on account of these experiences. But I must confess that they have transformed me, for better or for worse, both spiritually and intellectually. They have taught me new ways of relating to the divine as well as stimulated me to examine anew traditional Catholic teachings on non-Christian religions.

40

Three Important Things

Frederick Buechner

When Henry James was saying goodbye once to his young nephew Billy, his brother William's son, he said something that the boy never forgot. And of all the labyrinthine and impenetrably subtle things that that most labyrinthine and impenetrable old romancer could have said, what he did say was this: "There are three things that are important in human life. The first is to be kind. The second is to be kind. The third is to be kind."

Be kind because although kindness is not by a long shot the same thing as holiness, kindness is one of the doors that holiness enters the world through, enters us through—not just gently kind but sometimes fiercely kind.

Be kind enough to yourselves not just to play it

safe with your lives for your own sakes but to spend at least part of your lives like drunken sailors—for God's sake, if you believe in God, for the world's sake, if you believe in the world—and thus to come alive truly.

Be kind enough to others to listen, beneath all the words they speak, for that usually unspoken hunger for holiness which I believe is part of even the unlikeliest of us because by listening to it and cherishing it maybe we can help bring it to birth both in them and in ourselves.

41

Encounters with Kindness

William J. O'Malley, SJ

Despite what some might call twelve years of "Catholic brainwashing," many practicing Catholics persist in believing Christianity is limited to worshiping weekly and being moral—not hurting anybody, being polite, not fighting unless justified. But Christians have no monopoly on those. Good Jews and Moslems and even most good atheists want to be moral. Otherwise, you couldn't call them "good." But they're quite definitely not Christians.

Christians believe God became a human being, died a horrifying death, and returned to show that death is not the end. And his basic message at the Last Supper was that he broke himself up and handed round the pieces: "Do this in memory of me" and in everything else, beyond the Law, was that you have to care, especially for the outcasts, as Jesus—unarguably—did.

We ourselves are reluctant to be as vulnerable as God, because we see forgiveness of debts without penalty as at best poor business, and we don't want to look like patsies.

But God is a patsy. Matthew says (5:45) "God gives rain to those who are good and those who do evil." God gave us freedom to not love him, to act inhumanly. He gave freedom to an as yet imperfect set of apes. (Generous, not to mention risky.) And Jesus forgave without strings, without penances, without need to grovel. The only condition is that we come home.

The only question we face at the Final Judgment: "I was hungry. . . . I was thirsty. . . . I was a stranger. . . . I was naked. . . . I was sick. . . . I was in prison. . . ." What did you do? Mr. Rosewater captured it even more succinctly: "There's only one rule: Goddammit you've got to be kind."

When I was a kid, my Dad was in the food business with his uncle, Dan Murphy. They had three other drivers, and they would buy wholesale foods, break them down into affordable lots and sell them to Mom and Pop grocery stores. When Dan died, Dad took a partner named Tom Miles, whom my Mom didn't trust a bit. But Dad, who was the kindest soul I ever knew, said, "Bea, some people are honest."

Well, it turned out Mom was right. One Sunday, Miles decamped from Buffalo with his wife and two little daughters and the entire joint business bank account.

And Dad refused to call the police and prosecute.

His reason? "I don't want those two little girls growing up with their father a convict."

For a long time, I hated him for that. In high school, I had to take a morning paper route—which I hated, but which paid my tuition for four years' high school and two years' college and enabled me to buy my own clothes from eighth grade on. Fool that I was, I didn't realize how it made me grow up. Nor did I realize that Dad was a genuine Christian. He turned the other cheek; he walked the extra mile.

When I was a senior in high school, my Mom informed me that I was going to escort Kathleen Quinn to her senior prom. Now Kathleen lived only two blocks away and had been in my grammar school class eight years. She was the shyest girl God ever gave breath, and plain as a fence post. My instinct leaped immediately to my defense, and I was ready to say definitively that I was not going to escort Kathleen to her senior prom. However, that entailed saying "No" to my mother. Now Mom loved me with a love as primal as a she-wolf. However, one of her tasks was also to make me a young man of noblesse oblige and a Christian.

One time when I skipped my piano lesson to go with all my pals to the Saturday matinee movies, cartoons, and short subjects at the Kenmore Theater, I heard from the back of the darkened auditorium with about five hundred kids, "Where are you Bill O'Malley?" Down the aisle she strode, spotted me in the light spill from the screen, scrunched across the knees to grab me by the ear, scrunched back across the knees and up the aisle to my doom.

So, it goes without question that I did escort Kathleen Quinn to her prom. It was awful. I didn't have my night license, so my Dad had to drive us. It got worse. We got there on time. The only ones. I tried every conversational ploy—the band, the decorations, the causes of World War I. Nothing but a shy grin like a flower closing up for the night. It got worse. My sister had taught me to be a helluva good dancer. No one had taught Kathleen. Then my friends started to arrive with drop-dead gorgeous girls. Elbowing one another and jutting their chins in our direction. (I assumed.) As it drew near eleven-thirty, I said, "Well, it's getting late." So I called my Dad, and he picked us up and we took Kathleen home.

What a swine I was. It was almost surely her first date away from her strict family. Her first-ever party dress. And I spent the entire evening thinking of nothing but myself.

Since then, I directed fifty musicals, and I always made sure there was a handful of Kathleens sprinkled throughout the chorus.

It takes so little to be kind.

One rule I have for rehearsals when I direct plays is that, if you miss two rehearsals without giving me an excuse, you're out. I've never once actually put it into effect. If a boy or girl drops out they drop out. But I didn't let missing rehearsal go unnoticed. I'd call and find out what happened. One time, a boy missed two. So I cornered him at the beginning of class. I said, "Jimmy, anything you want to say to me?" He looked as if I'd asked the time and he didn't have a watch, then he suddenly realized. "Oh, about the rehearsals? Are you gonna kick me out?" I said, "No," and that really caught his attention. I said, "Jim, I'm just waiting for two words." A couple of tears came together in the corners of his eyes. "You mean, 'I'm . . . I'm sorry?'" I said, "If you really mean it."

The tears tumbled down, and to my shock, he threw his arms around me and said, "Oh I'm sorry, I'm really sorry. What can I do?" So I said, "I just want you to say those same two words to the whole cast this afternoon, and it's over. We'll never mention it again."

Neither of us will probably ever forget that. It made us both feel so good.

So this is what happens to both people when we forgive, relent—when we're kind.

A lot of the gospels show Jesus doing the same thing: going on the prowl for the Kathleens, and usually folks in far worse shape—lepers, societal rejects like whores and grafters, and twelve apostles who took forever to understand just what he was inviting them to do themselves—go out and find the stray sheep and bring them home.

42

10 Ways to Deepen Your Loving-Kindness Practice

Sharon Salzberg

1. *Think of kindness as a strength, not as a weakness.* Kindness isn't an ally of foolishness or gullibility, but rather an ally of wisdom and courage.

2. *Look for the good in yourself*—not as a way to deny your difficulties or problems but as a way to broaden your outlook so it's more truthful and balanced. Looking for the good in ourselves helps us see the good in others.

3. *Remember that everyone wants to be happy.* If we look deeply into any kind of behavior, we will see an urge to feel a part of something greater than our own limited sense of self, a desire to feel at home in this body and mind. This urge toward happiness

is often twisted and distorted by ignorance, by not knowing where happiness is actually to be found. Remembering what we share inspires us toward kindness.

4. *Recollect those who have helped or inspired us.* Sometimes even a small act of kindness on someone's part makes an essential difference for us. Cultivating gratitude is a way of honoring these people, and also a way of lifting our spirits and reminding us of the power of good-heartedness.

5. *Practice at least one act of generosity a day.* We all have something to give, large or small. It may be a smile, or an attentive conversation. Perhaps you let a stranger get ahead of you in line, or gave a coworker a small gift, or wrote a late-night note of appreciation. Any act of generosity—whether material or of the spirit—is a meaningful expression of kindness.

6. *Do loving-kindness meditation.* Each day we can take the time to hold others in our hearts quietly and wish them well. This meditation might include someone who has been helpful or inspiring to us, someone we know who is feeling alone or afraid, someone who is experiencing triumph and joy, or someone we are about to meet with some

trepidation. We might, depending on the circumstances of our lives, particularly include children or animals in our thoughts. Taking just 10 minutes a day to reflect in this way is a powerful path to transformation.

7. *Listen.* Often we have conversations where we are only partially paying attention; we're thinking about the next e-mail we need to send, or what we forgot to mention to the last person we spoke to. Or we decide we know what the other person is going to say, based on past encounters. Reopening that closed file by listening is a powerful gesture of kindness, one that allows fresh responses and transformed relationships.

8. *Include those who seem left out.* In a conversation with a group of people, there may be those too shy to speak. In a room full of partygoers, there may be some who feel out of place. Be the one who opens the circle.

9. *Refrain from speaking ill of others.* A friend told me about a time he resolved not to talk about any third person; if he had something to say about someone, he would say it directly to that person instead. If you feel tempted to put someone down, assume knowledge of their bad motives, or generally prove

their inferiority, take a breath. Even though we might feel a rush of power in saying those words, we ultimately get no benefit from dividing people and sowing seeds of dissension and dislike. There are ways to talk about wrong behavior without derision or condemnation.

10. *"Walk a mile in another person's shoes before you pass judgment."* As this old saying suggests, even if we're going to take strong action to try to change someone's behavior, a sense of empathy and understanding for them won't weaken us. If anything, that element of kindness will allow us to act more compassionately and creatively.

43

Two Cups of Coffee—
"One on the Wall"

Anonymous

I sat with my friend in a well-known coffee shop in a neighboring town of Venice, Italy, the city of lights and water.

As we enjoyed our coffee, a man entered and sat at an empty table beside us. He called the waiter and placed his order saying, "Two cups of coffee, one of them there on the wall."

We heard this order with rather interest and observed that he was served with one cup of coffee but he paid for two.

When he left, the waiter put a piece of paper on the wall saying "A Cup of Coffee."

While we were still there, two other men entered

and ordered three cups of coffee, two on the table and one on the wall. They had two cups of coffee but paid for three and left. This time also, the waiter did the same; he put a piece of paper on the wall saying, "A Cup of Coffee."

It was something unique and perplexing for us. We finished our coffee, paid the bill and left.

After a few days, we had a chance to go to this coffee shop again. While we were enjoying our coffee, a man poorly dressed entered. As he seated himself, he looked at the wall and said, "One cup of coffee from the wall."

The waiter served coffee to this man with the customary respect and dignity. The man had his coffee and left without paying.

We were amazed to watch all this, as the waiter took off a piece of paper from the wall and threw it in the trash bin.

Now it was no surprise for us—the matter was very clear. The great respect for the needy shown by the inhabitants of this town made our eyes well up in tears.

A truly beautiful thought. Probably the most beautiful wall you may ever see anywhere!

Kindly Light

"Hello, babies. Welcome to Earth. It's hot in the summer and cold in the winter. It's round and wet and crowded. On the outside, babies, you've got a hundred years here. There's only one rule that I know of, babies—God damn it, you've got to be kind."

—KURT VONNEGUT

Sources and Acknowledgments

Orbis Books has made every effort to identify the owner of each selection in this book, and to obtain permission from the author, publisher, or agent in question. In the event of inadvertent errors, please notify us.

1. Michael Blumenthal, "Be Kind," from *No Hurry: Poems 2000–2012*. Copyright © 2012 by Michael Blumenthal. Wilkes-Barre, PA: Etruscan Press, 2012. Reprinted by permission of Etruscan Press.

2. Anne Lamott, "Destination Kindness," from *Hallelujah Anyway: Rediscovering Mercy*. Copyright © 2017 by Anne Lamott. Used by permission of Riverhead, an imprint of Penguin Publishing Group, a division of Penguin Random House and The Wylie Agency LLC. All rights reserved.

3. Joan Chittister, "Memories of Unkindness," from *Illuminated Life: Monastic Wisdom for Seekers of Light*, Maryknoll, NY: Orbis Books, 2000.

4. Amy Morris-Young, "My Acts of Kindness Always Yield Craziness," originally published by *National Catholic Reporter*. NCRonline.org, November 24, 2016. Reprinted by permission of Amy Morris-Young and *National Catholic Reporter*.

5. Mother Teresa, "The Evidence of Kindness," from www.awesomestories.com, November 17, 2015.

6. Thich Nhat Hanh, "I am Sorry, I will Never Do That Again," from "The Practice of Loving Kindness," excerpted from *The Four Mantras* as found on mindfulnessbell.org/archive, Dharma Talk: True Presence, #15 Winter 1995. Reprinted by permission of *The Mindfulness Bell*.

7. George Saunders, "Err on the Side of Kindness," from *Congratulations, By the Way: Some Thoughts on Kindness*. Copyright © 2014 by George Saunders. Used by permission of Random House, an

imprint and division of Penguin Random House LLC. All rights reserved.

8. Kerry Weber, "Learning to Love My Neighbor in New York," excerpted from *Mercy in the City: How to Feed the Hungry, Give Drink to the Thirsty, Visit the Imprisoned, and Keep Your Day Job*. Chicago: Loyola Press, 2014. Copyright © 2014 by Kerry Weber. Reprinted with permission of Loyola Press. To order copies visit www.loyolapress.com.

9. Emily Esfahani Smith, "Masters of Love," copyright © 2014 The Atlantic Media Co., as first published in *The Atlantic Magazine*. All rights reserved. Distributed by Tribune Content Agency, LLC.

10. Richard Rohr, "My Religion Is Kindness," from *Richard Rohr's Daily Meditation*, Friday, January 3, 2014. Used with permission.

11. Naomi Shihab Nye, "The Tender Gravity of Kindness," originally published as "Kindness" in *Words Under the Words: Selected Poems (A Far Corner Book)*. Copyright © 1994 by Naomi Shihab Nye. Portland, OR: The Eighth Mountain Press, 1994. Reprinted by permission of Far Corner Books.

12. Jack Kornfield, "A Meditation on Lovingkindness," from *The Art of Forgiveness, Lovingkindness, and Peace*. Copyright © 2017 by Jack Kornfield. All Rights Reserved. Reprinted by permission of Jack Kornfield.

13. Joyce Rupp, "Look for Unannounced Angels," from *Walk in a Relaxed Manner*. Maryknoll, NY: Orbis Books, 2005.

14. Joseph G. Healey, "I Had Lunch with God," from *Once Upon a Time in Africa: Stories of Wisdom & Joy*, compiled by Joseph G. Healey. Maryknoll, NY: Orbis Books, 2004.

15. Dorothy Day, "In Praise of the Crushed Heart," adapted from "The Scandal of the Works of Mercy," *Commonweal*, 1949, as reprinted in *Dorothy Day: Selected Writings*, Robert Ellsberg, ed. Maryknoll, NY: Orbis Books, 2005.

Sources and Acknowledgments

16. Pope Francis, "A Path toward Sainthood," excerpt from Pope Francis's General Audience, Wednesday, November 19, 2014. Copyright © Libreria Editrice Vaticana. Reprinted by permission of Libreria Editrice Vaticana.

17. Terry Golway, "Building a Bridge with Kind Words," from *America Magazine,* June 23, 2003. Reprinted by permission of Terry Golway.

18. Michael Leach, "People Will Always Be Kind," originally published by *National Catholic Reporter;* NCRonline.org, November 4, 2017.

19. Jack Kerouac, "Practice Kindness All Day to Everybody," from a January 28, 1957, letter to Edith Parker Kerouac, collected in *Selected Letters 1957–1969* by Jack Kerouac. Copyright © 1957 Jack Kerouac, 1999 Estate of Stella Kerouac, used by permission of The Wylie Agency LLC.

20. James Martin, SJ, "Don't Be a Jerk," from *America Magazine,* April 18, 2016. Reprinted by permission of James Martin.

21. Michael Schulman, "Stuck in Gander" from *The New Yorker*, March 27, 2017. Reprinted by permission of Condé Nast.

22. Carlo Carretto, "Love Is for Living," from *Love Is for Living.* Maryknoll, NY: Orbis Books, 1976.

23. Henry Morgenthau, III, "A Sunday in Purgatory," from *A Sunday in Purgatory*, Passager Books, 2016. Reprinted by permission of Passager Books.

24. Henri Nouwen, "Becoming Kind," from *Bread for the Journey: A Daybook of Wisdom and Faith.* Copyright © 1997 by Henri J. M. Nouwen. Reprinted by permission of HarperCollins Publishers.

25. James H. Kroeger, MM, "Ten Commandments of Kindness," originally published as "Living Kindness: Everyday Virtue" in *East Asian Pastoral Review* 46, no. 4 (2009). Reprinted by permission of James H. Kroeger.

26. M.J. Riordan, "Bear One Another's Burden," originally published as "Bear Ye One Another's Burden" in *The America Book of Verse*. New York: America Press, 1928.

27. Joseph G. Healey, "The Two Brothers," true story from Sukuma ethnic group, Tanzania, collected by the Sukuma Research Committee, Bujora, Tanzania, as reprinted in *Once Upon a Time in Africa: Stories of Wisdom & Joy*, compiled by Joseph G. Healey. Maryknoll, NY: Orbis Books, 2004.

28. John Shea, "My Mother's Best Putt," from *Stories by John Shea*. Copyright © 2008 by John Shea. Chicago: ACTA Publishers, 2008. www.actapublications.com. Used with permission. All rights reserved.

29. Steve Hartman, "Man Proves, Once Again, That Kindness Can Be a Calling," from CBSNews.com, April 7, 2017. Reprinted by permission of CBS News Archives.

30. Victor Hugo, "The Bishop's Candlesticks," from *Les Misérables*. Adapted and translated by William J. O'Malley.

31. O. Henry, "The Last Leaf," reprinted from online-literature.com. Originally published in *The Trimmed Lamp and Other Stories*. Garden City, NY: Doubleday, Page & Co., 1907.

32. T.S. Arthur, "An Angel in Disguise," reprinted from americanliterature.com.

33. Barbara E. Reid, "The Kindness of Strangers," from *America Magazine*, July 5, 2010. Reprinted by permission of Barbara E. Reid.

34. Dorothy Day, "We Are Trying to Make People Happy," from *The Third Hour*, 1949, as reprinted in *Dorothy Day: Selected Writings*, Robert Ellsberg ed. Maryknoll, NY: Orbis Books, 2005.

35. Peter Schineller, "Try a Little Kindness," from *America Magazine*, March 2, 2009. Reprinted by permission of Peter Schineller.

36. Jessica Powers, "My Heart Ran Forth," from *The Selected Poetry of*

Jessica Powers. Washington, DC: ICS Publications, 1999. All copyrights, Carmelite Monastery, Pewaukee, WI. Used with permission.

37. Michael Leach, "Bishop Morrie Says It's Not about the Soup," originally published by *National Catholic Reporter;* NCRonline.org, July, 2015.

38. Kelli M. Wheeler, "What Have You Done for Someone Today?" from www.momservations.com, July 27, 2016. Used by permission of Kelli M. Wheeler.

39. Peter Phan, "Blessings of Kindness," from *The Joy of Religious Pluralism.* Maryknoll, NY: Orbis Books, 2017.

40. Frederick Buechner, "Three Important Things," from "Growing Up," address published in *The Clown in the Belfry.* HarperSanFrancisco, 1992. Reprinted by permission of Frederick Buechner Literary Asset, LLC.

41. William J. O'Malley, SJ, "Encounters with Kindness." Reprinted by permission of William J. O'Malley.

42. Sharon Salzberg, "10 Ways to Deepen Your Loving-Kindness Practice," excerpted from *Real Happiness.* Copyright © 2011 by Sharon Salzberg. Used by permission of Workman Publishing Co., Inc., New York. All Rights Reserved.

43. Anonymous, "Two Cups of Coffee—'One on the Wall' " from www.spiritual-short-stories.com.

INDEX OF CONTRIBUTORS

T.S. Arthur (d. 1885) was a nineteenth-century American magazine publisher and author, most famous for his novel *Ten Nights in a Bar-Room and What I Saw There* (1854) and his stories for *Godey's Lady's Book*, a popular American magazine in the antebellum era..... **32**

Michael Blumenthal is the author of several poetry collections, including *No Hurry: Poems 2000–2012* and *Dusty Angel*, which won the Isabella Steward Gardner Prize......................... **1**

Frederick Buechner is a Presbyterian minister and the author of more than thirty books across numerous genres. His book *Godric* was a finalist for the 1981 Pulitzer Prize...................... **40**

Carlo Carretto (d. 1988) was a member of the Little Brothers of Jesus, a religious order inspired by the spirituality of Charles de Foucauld, and the author of more than a dozen books, including the bestselling *Letters from the Desert*............................ **22**

Joan Chittister, OSB, is a popular religious writer and the award-winning author of *The Way of the Cross, For Everything a Season, The Way We Were*, and many other books. She is a member of the Benedictines in Erie, Pennsylvania. **3**

Dorothy Day (d. 1980) was the founder of the Catholic Worker movement and one of the most prophetic voices in the American Catholic Church in the twentieth century. Her canonization cause is currently proceeding in the Archdiocese of New York..... **15, 34**

Pope Francis is the current pontiff of the Roman Catholic Church. **16**

Terry Golway is a professor at Kean University and a former columnist for the *New York Times*. He is the author of several books on Irish and American history, including *JFK: Day by Day*......... **17**

Steve Hartman has been a CBS News Correspondent based in New York since 1998. His award-winning feature segment "On the

Index of Contributors

The Way of Kindness